James Edwin Thorold Rogers

Rabbi Jeshua, an Eastern Story

James Edwin Thorold Rogers
Rabbi Jeshua, an Eastern Story
ISBN/EAN: 9783743383883
Manufactured in Europe, USA, Canada, Australia, Japa
Cover: Foto ©Lupo / pixelio.de

Manufactured and distributed by brebook publishing software (www.brebook.com)

James Edwin Thorold Rogers

Rabbi Jeshua, an Eastern Story

RABBI JESHUA.

RABBI JESHUA

AN EASTERN STORY

"Write me as one that loves his fellow-men."

LONDON
C. KEGAN PAUL & CO., 1, PATERNOSTER SQUARE
1881

INTRODUCTION.

THE present volume is intended to present, as clearly as may be possible, considering the scantiness of the original materials, the history of a brief but of an eventful career.

It is true that rabbinical literature presents attractions only to the few. One of our popular writers has confessed that even when undertaking so serious a task as the compilation of a Life of Christ, he did not consider it necessary to master the three stout folios which comprise the Mishna, or text of the Talmud ; and in common with others he has condemned the study of this early Jewish work—the epitome of law, custom, and belief among the Hebrews—as belonging to a literature which is quite unworthy the notice of a serious scholar.

Yet in spite of these dicta of modern authorities there are few stories more fascinating or pathetic than that of the loving, passionate, devoted life which it is here proposed to describe; and it may perhaps prove capable, when shorn of the quaint conceits of the original Hebrew chronicle, and when illustrated by contemporary literature, of attracting a wider circle of readers than that composed of rabbinical students. It is a narrative so intensely human, so independent of merely local colour, so noble and true in spite of the prejudices and ignorance of the chronicler, that wherever the love of truth exists it must surely find an attentive audience.

There are many sources whence information may be drawn. The apochryphal accounts of Rabbi Jeshua's life written in the Middle Ages have however no value or interest; and although about a dozen lives of the Rabbi were composed by his followers within a century after his death, the spirit of the writer, rather than that of the master himself, is, as a rule, reflected in each. The views which are ascribed to Rabbi Jeshua in these works are so diametrically opposed to one another, and so self-contradictory, as to make it clear to the critical reader that the disciples mingled their own teaching with that of their master, and ranked their own views as of equal importance with his; that they placed their own words in his mouth, and their own construction on his actions.

One chronicle is often attributed to Rabbi Saul, pupil of Gamaliel, and a native of Asia Minor. A second breathes the spirit of the narrow Pharisaic sect of Shammai. A third, written by an Alexandrine Jew, is full of Cabbalistic lore and of Egyptian mysticism. Rabbi Jeshua cannot have belonged to all these schools at once, and when we find the various accounts of his actions to be equally contrary in the various versions, we are led to suppose that but little remains on which we can safely rely.

Most of these works may perhaps be best regarded as originally written for controversial purposes. The object of the Jerusalem version is clearly that of showing how Rabbi Jeshua fulfilled in every respect the Pharisaic expectations of a Messiah. The book of Rabbi Saul, on the other hand, breathes the liberal spirit of the opposite party of Hillel and Gamaliel, and introduces many latitudinarian views probably held by the writer himself rather than by the master to whom he attributes them. Our appreciation of the poetic beauties and truths of this composition, as well as of those which may be discovered hidden among the repulsive mysticisms of the Alexandrine version, is a sentiment entirely distinct from the question of authorship. To us in the nineteenth century it perhaps matters little whether the thoughts expressed owe their origin to Rabbi Jeshua, or to one of his followers; but with regard to the incidents of his career, it is at least necessary to sift the evidence, and to endeavour to discover the true facts of his life.

It is for this reason that the following pages are principally based on a short and succinct account of the life of Rabbi Jeshua, which was written by the companion of one of his first disciples, Simeon has Saddik. Simeon himself was an illiterate peasant, a man probably older than Rabbi Jeshua, but who survived him more than forty years, and retired before the fall of Jerusalem to the neighbourhood of Gadara, east of Jordan.

The recollections of this aged puritan were recorded by one of his companions. The historical sequence of the events appears to have been carefully followed, and many of the maxims of Rabbi Jeshua are preserved, interspersed among descriptions of the main events of his short career. Thus, though scanty and imperfect, the information contained in this work appears to be genuine ; and it has evidently served as the original basis of the other accounts, for this reason, that in no case do they agree in any statement which contradicts one made by Simeon has Saddik. All the versions are in agreement when they follow that which may be considered to be the original, and on the other hand no two of the later versions are in accord concerning facts not noticed by Simeon. Thus we have the indication of genuineness in the one case and of fanciful elaboration in all the others, and our attention should be confined to those statements which have the best right to be considered truthful because they are found to be common to every version.

The brief chronicle which bears the name of Simeon has Saddik is nevertheless not free from serious defects as an historic work. Though evidently written after the fall of Jerusalem it attributes to Rabbi Jeshua a prophecy of that event, and thus incurs the suspicion of belonging to the large class of Jewish apocalypic literature which abounds with pretended prophecies of past events, a kind of composition which, though probably never intended to deceive, is often branded by modern critics with the name of forgery. It is also clear that the ignorance and credulity of the peasant disciple, though a man of vigorous and affectionate nature, has incapacitated him in many cases for rightly appreciating the lessons and motives of his master. The superstitious beliefs of the age find frequent expression in the pages of this chronicle, but it is by no means clear that they were credited of Rabbi Jeshua. The chronicle of Simeon has nevertheless this advantage over the other versions, that the number of its miracles is smaller; and it is clear that an original account written by a European (had such an account been possible) would have been entirely free from the supernatural element. As, however, no such document exists, we must make the best use of the genuine material available, discounting, as far as possible, the idiosyncrasies of the writer, and striving to form some kind of idea of the actual facts which he relates.

In concluding these introductory remarks it may be noted that there is nothing in the life which we are about to study which would appear extraordinary or impossible if the events were supposed to have happened in our own times, so long as the scene was laid, not in Europe, but in Asia.

So unchangeable is the East, that the sentiments of the modern Oriental reproduce, almost unchanged, the ideas and motives of the Jew of nineteen centuries since. The loss of the feeling of reverence which characterises the civilisation of the West has never occurred in the native home of the monotheistic faiths. Were Rabbi Jeshua to be re-born in the England of to-day it would probably be his fate to be imprisoned as a vagabond and an impostor; but were he, on the other hand, to revisit his native land he would find but little change in the character of the peasantry whom he loved, and but little loss of the religious instinct which is still distinctive of the reverent and reverend East.

CONTENTS.

CHAPTER		PAGE
I.	Hebrew Hermits	1
II.	Who was Rabbi Jeshua?	15
III.	Society in the Tetrarchies	30
IV.	The Hope of the People	52
V.	Rabbi Jeshua's Life	68
VI.	Sayings of Rabbi Jeshua	95
VII.	The Death of Rabbi Jeshua	124
VIII.	Legendary History	151
IX.	England and Rabbi Jeshua	171

RABBI JESHUA.

CHAPTER I.

HEBREW HERMITS.

The Jordan valley—Hanan of Bethania—Monasticism among the Jews—The Hasaya or "pious"—The doctrines of Hanan—Prophets modern and ancient—Political power of prophets—Fate of Hanan.

An open river valley carpeted with luxuriant herbage and gay with wild flowers. On either side a steep shapeless ridge of dark grey limestone scarred with winter torrent beds and stained with rusty patches of colour. In the distance are black precipices of basalt and white peaks of marl worn by the rain into fantastic forms. A snowy mountain dome closes the view, a sky of burning blue arches it over. In the middle of the flat valley runs the great trench a mile wide and a hundred feet deep, which has been worn by the river. Steep banks of gleaming marl flank the lower valley, through which the stream winds its way in a serpentine course. Scattered thorn trees, a few stunted palms, and huge thistles ten to fifteen feet in height, form the most conspicuous objects on the upper plateau; but round the river itself, and on the islets in its midst a thick jungle of cane and brown tamarisk almost conceals from view the rapid swirling current of grey water which slips by, brimming over the flowery margin of the channel.

The silence of the desert broods over this wild yet luxuriant valley. The note of the singing bird is not heard, nor the sighing of the wind in trees. The cry of the eagle or the bark of the jackal alone breaks the stillness of the solitude, and for perhaps a fortnight in spring the green prairie is flecked with white as the solemn storks descend for a time to rest on their way beside the springs.

Yet down beside the river itself a human voice is heard crying in the wilderness, and a crowd of eager listeners surround the wild figure of the preacher.

Clad in a rough mantle, girt with a broad leather belt, his jetty curls, unshorn since his birth, hang on his shoulders in elf locks mingling with his scanty beard. A sun-scorched complexion bears witness to the rude life of the dweller in the desert, and the striking beauty of the features marks the pure caste of a priestly family.

Around the hermit are gathered the inhabitants of city and village, some of whom have come from a distance of several days' journey. Sleek rabbis from Jerusalem, fierce Roman mercenaries and native auxiliaries, poor peasants and fishermen from Galilee, prosperous mechanics from Sepphoris or Scythopolis, tax-gatherers and officials, ploughmen and shepherds, all eager to listen to the prophet whose austere life and bitter denunciations were famous through the length and breadth of the land.

The hermit whom we have thus described, though perhaps one of the most prominent members of his sect, was not, however, a unique example of his kind. The natural impulse of contemplative minds to separate from their fellows was not less powerfully felt in Judea than it has been in other lands. As civilisation increased, and the exigencies of Jewish life became more complicated, the observation of many archaic institutions of the law became almost impossible for the townsman. Thus in the later Hasmonean times and during the Herodian age we find a sect of Therapeutæ springing up in Palestine and attaining a reputation for sanctity and supernatural powers, which was the natural inference from a retired and austere life in the minds of an awe-stricken and superstitious populace.

As among the early hermits of Egypt or of our own islands, so among the Hebrews, this movement resulted partly in the creation of religious confraternities—the precursors of the great orders of Christian monks—and partly in the retirement of individual eremites to the solitude of the wilderness. Pliny informs us that the deserts surrounding the Dead Sea were inhabited by these recluses, who thus formed the prototypes of the famous Saba and his companions, dwelling in caves among the fastnesses of the Kedron valley. Josephus describes the life of the early hermit Banu, or Bunai, who dwelt in the wilderness and was clothed only with leaves or rushes, while his food consisted of wild berries and fruits. Day and night he performed frequent ablutions in the cold water of the mountain springs, and spent his hours in meditation and prayer.

To the same class belonged the semi-monastic sects of the Abionim (or "poor") and the Hasaya (or "pious"), the second of which is first mentioned in the time of John Hyrcanus, about 140 B.C. Owning no settled habitation in any city, the ascetic dwelt in a common home with his brethren, and had all things in common with them. Stewards were appointed at these monasteries, as well as brethren who sheltered the travelling members when passing from one station to another. Silence, chastity, obedience, and poverty, were the rules of the order. Swearing was forbidden, and a noviciate had to be first passed before the aspirant was admitted to the four higher degrees.

In all these respects the Jewish religious orders were indistinguishable from the monks and hermits of a later age. Like them, they were engaged in the study of medicine, in religious duties, and in agriculture. They were vowed to asceticism, and wore a distinctive girdle and robe of white. Even in the Syria of our own times, some echo of the same spirit is observable among the Druses, whose rules of initiation and of retreat to the desert recall those of the Jewish ascetics.

The religious creed of the Hasaya was, however, distinctive, and in some respects departed from the strict orthodoxy of the original Law. They neglected the prescribed sacrifices, and the annual visits to Jerusalem; they encouraged celibacy; which was a clear dereliction from the primary duty inculcated in the very commencement of the Holy Torah, "to increase and multiply." They attached especial importance to frequent ablutions;

and baptism became the distinctive ceremony of the sect. They are even said to have held certain mystic tenets connected with sun worship and the belief in angels, which are certainly not traceable to the law of Moses.

As physicians, the fame of the Hasaya was widely spread. Prophecies were attributed by common tradition to many members of their sect, and some of these are stated to have been fulfilled in a remarkable manner. As regarded the future they were complete fatalists, but believed in the immortality of the soul and in a future heaven and hell.

Thus, although in the eyes of the most rigidly orthodox these religious orders may have appeared to depart from the strict observance of the Law, and to have been liable to the stigma of heresy, there is no doubt that by the common people, and even by their rulers, they were regarded with a veneration amounting almost to awe, and resulting from the seclusion and sanctity of their lives, not less than from their reputation for skill in medicine, and for knowledge of mysterious arts.

Such, then, was Hanan of Bethania, the Hebrew hermit of the Jordan valley. As a member of the sect of Hasaya, he inculcated the duty of washing in cold water as conducive to chastity. As a prophet, he exhorted his hearers to penitence and good works, through which the ardently expected coming of Messiah might be quickened ; for, like Rabbi Judah, nearly two centuries later, he taught that, through the conversion of Israel, the great future might be hastened, and that the calculation of days and weeks, of times and years, was but a vain waste of human ingenuity, so long as the hearts of the disobedient were not turned to the wisdom of the just.

At a period subsequent to his death, Hanan was regarded as the forerunner of Messiah—the mysterious re-incarnate Elijah. To this belief we must refer later ; but it is here sufficient to note that he does not himself appear to have laid claim to this mystic character, and that by Josephus he is mentioned only as an ascetic, and a preacher having an unusual influence with the people.

Wandering by the banks of the winding Jordan; crying aloud in the great gorges through which the tributary streams flow from east and west to join the river ; sheltered by night in the caves which nature has blasted in the rough hill-sides ; fed by the wild bees, or the locust swarms, like the nomad Arabs among whom he dwelt, the hermit of Bethania passed his life in denunciation, in exhortation, in the purifying rites of frequent washings, in the mortification of the body, in fasting and prayer.

Even by his contemporaries, Hanan was considered as a prophet. It was the gift which in the belief of the populace specially distinguished his sect; and the prediction of the coming of Messiah was the burden of his exhortations.

In all ages the Eastern peoples have believed in the existence of prophets living in their midst. Not only in the Herodian period, or when Akiba roused the flame of fanaticism at Bether, but down through the dark ages and the mediæval period, throughout the later history of Judaism, we find the appearance of new prophets greeted by believing crowds. In our own days the Moslem holds a similar faith in the inspiration of living prophets.

The naked dervish, wandering from village to village, living on alms and trading on the superstitious terrors of the ignorant, is the prophet of the peasantry. The sleek mollah whose writings are disseminated among the educated, who proclaims the future triumph of Islam over Western civilisation, and denounces the devices of the Christian infidel, is the prophet of the rich and great. The belief in the supernatural, in possession, inspiration, the constant interference of the unseen powers, is still an active element of daily life in the East. By such influences all that is strange or unusual in occurrence is easily explained, and, save perhaps among spiritualists, we have in the West no class which thus lives in imagination, surrounded with spells and controlled by occult powers; no race whose daily actions are in like manner practically influenced by a belief in the invisible world.

It is hard to realise the results of this familiarity with the idea of the supernatural so universal among Orientals, so rare among Western peoples. We are apt at once to overrate, and yet to undercalculate, the power of prophets among the Hebrews. We attach an amount of dignity to the character of the seer far beyond that which properly belongs to it; for we have no prophets among ourselves, and we forget that in the East many prophets are still to be found.

The modern dervish, no doubt, presents the closest parallel which still exists to the Hebrew prophet of old. The poet, the madman, the enthusiast, receive, as of yore, the reverent homage of a simple folk; and false prophets were not less commonly found among the Jews (as they themselves admitted) than are charlatans and impostors among the fanatics who have attained in the Syria of to-day to a reputation for sanctity.

Preceded by the pipe and the tabret, the holy man wanders as a pilgrim through the country. Sometimes he may be seen writhing under an ecstasy which seems produced by fanatical excitement. He foams at the mouth, uttering strange cries, and wounding himself with knives or swords like the prophets of Baal on Carmel. He will, perhaps, undertake to strike a bystander with a sharp sword without producing a wound, or will charm serpents from their holes, and devour scorpions without injury.

Neither fire nor poison nor the stroke of cold steel can harm his charmed existence, and the faithful will relate tales of his miraculous powers, of those whose prayer he has heard and answered, while himself many miles away, or of his acquaintance with the deeds and history of others on whom he sets eyes for the first time.

So long as the exhortations of the modern prophet are confined to abstract principles of morality, so long as he denounces only the enemies of the existing power, his life may be passed in enjoyment of a high reputation without any interference on the part of those who govern the land.

If, indeed, the local ruler be himself of a pious or a superstitious character, the prophet may be found seated in the council chamber, and though ragged and poor, will be treated with a respect greater than is shown by the host to his more wealthy and better-born guests.

Occasions may however arise when the enthusiast is directly opposed to the rulers of the land. The court religion may be that of Baal, the faith of the prophet that of Jehovah. In such a case he must try his strength against the established powers, and he becomes suddenly a person of the highest political importance. It was thus that Elijah swayed the multitude, and earned the undying hatred of Jezebel. It was thus that Rabbi Akiba raised the standard of revolt against Rome, and deluged the mountains of Bether with Jewish blood. It is thus that in our own times we may see the mollah or the dervish spread the green banner which proclaims war against the perverted pasha not less than against the Christian kafir. The enthusiasm for national faith, which is in the East the counterpart of Western patriotism, may thus at times make a revolutionist of the prophet; yet it is from impulse and conviction, rather than from principle and design, that Orientals ever act, and it would be entirely wrong to brand the popular leader as a scheming politician when he is in his own eyes acting under direct inspiration, and in obedience to the highest motives, moral and religious.

The power which Hanan the hermit exercised over the populace was of this peculiar character. He had himself no political aspirations, and acted only from a firm belief in the coming Divine interference, which should change the established order of things. Yet in the eyes of the Idumean monarch, whose hold on the affections of the nation was weakened by his foreign birth and his semi-pagan tendencies, Hanan could not but become obnoxious as a possible leader of some revolutionary movement.

A native prince might be found claiming descent from the house of David; he might be accepted by the populace, and exhorted by the prophet to enforce his claims: the visionary Messiah might become a flesh and blood reality, and a movement based on the deep religious feeling of the Jewish nation might drive the Roman and the Idumean alike from the land.

The catastrophe caused by such fears was not long delayed. For how many years Hanan preached in the desert is not known, but he received at length the courteous request to present himself before the ruler of Galilee and Perea, by which the crafty Antipas concealed his design of quietly forestalling the possibility of revolt. Welcomed at the court with a respect due to the holiness of his character, he was detained to exhort the monarch, and boldly reproved him for the licence of his life. Whether it were through the influence of those women on whom his denunciations fell most bitterly, or by reason of the alarm which was excited by the rapid growth of his reputation and fame among the Jews, it is certain that he was never again allowed to wander in freedom among his familiar deserts. In the gloomy fortress which looks down from the rugged eastern cliffs upon the gleaming oily waters of the Bitter Sea, Hanan pined in captivity, cheered only by the furtive visits of his most attached disciples. At length, when his imprisonment was no longer remembered by the mass of the people, his execution was secretly ordered, and Antipas succeeded, while thus ridding himself of a dangerous enemy, in casting the blame on others, and in himself appearing to regret a deed forced upon him against his will.

In thus relating the fate of the hermit, we have, however, somewhat forestalled the order of our narrative, for it was whilst Hanan was still preaching and prophesying at Bethania that Rabbi Jeshua first appeared prominently in public, and became a convert to the sect of the Hasaya. Conspicuous among the crowd, and already famous for his piety and learning, this great man was the most important convert that Hanan ever made; but, on the other hand, the influence of the ascetic on his pupil was not less important in moulding the character and influencing the fate of one who was afterwards destined so far to outstrip his master.

CHAPTER II.

WHO WAS RABBI JESHUA?

Modern paraphrases—Contradictory legends—A Galilean school—Jewish education—Rabbi Jeshua's boyhood—Retreat to the desert.

IT is related of Doctor Johnson that he once opened a paraphrase of the Gospels, and found the shortest verse in the Bible, "Jesus wept," elaborated into the sentence, "The Saviour of mankind melted into a flood of tears." "Puppy," cried the doctor in his wrath, and flung the volume into the fire.

It was, however, easier for the great critic to destroy a worthless book than it would be to stamp out that natural love of filling in with vivid colouring the meagre outlines of biography which seems to characterise the modern historian. Even of the New Testament narrative we have more than one reproduction, which amplifies in flowery verbiage the terse and poetic language of the Hebrew author, and which dilutes the curt narrative with a fanciful, an inaccurate, and often a sentimental commentary, more remarkable for its orthodoxy than for the originality of its reflections. Have we not the beautifully illustrated work of Canon Farrar, and the yet larger book of Geikie? Has not the life of John the Baptist been elaborated so as to fill a volume? Have we not even now amongst us the descendants of that puppy with whom the honest doctor was so wroth, who tell us in sixteen pages of print the fact stamped on our memories by the half-dozen words which have been familiar to us from childhood?

Of all periods which interest the biographer, that of the infancy and childhood of his hero is probably the most fascinating. To record the earliest indications of genius, the first gleams of beauty in the mind, the gradual development of a noble character, is a task in which the true student of human nature must ever delight; and this desire to trace back the life history of a great man to his childhood is not less remarkable among the primitive biographers of Rabbi Jeshua than among the Geikies or the Farrars of our own time.

The honest chronicle of Simeon has Saddik does not, however, attempt any such task. Whether the parentage and ancestry of Rabbi Jeshua were unknown to his humble follower, or whether the subject was considered of small importance by the disciple, the fact remains that the biography commences only at that point where its hero first presented himself to the notice of the world; and that not a single word of preface or explanation is therein given, to record, however briefly, the birth and early life of the great Rabbi.

It is true that in the later accounts of Rabbi Jeshua's life some attempts have been made to remedy this deficiency; but these stories belong rather to the category of legend than to that of actual history, and their want of authenticity is indicated by two peculiarities, namely: first, the introduction of the marvellous element, and the use of supernatural machinery; secondly, the mutually contradictory character of the legends themselves.

Thus in the Pharisaic account of Rabbi Jeshua's life we find the statement that he was born at Bethlehem, south of Jerusalem—a statement which might appear unaccountable in view of the fact that he was a Galilean, were it not evident that an apologetic work, which sought to prove the Messianic claim of the Rabbi, must of necessity conform to the popular belief that Messiah should be born in the city of David.

According then to the tradition of the Jerusalem

C

school, Rabbi Jeshua was born in the little rock-cut stable adjoining the village inn — a grotto, similar to the innumerable cave stables which are burrowed in the hill-sides, round Bethlehem, or on the slopes above the desert, where David once watched his father's flocks.

But there was yet another prophecy to be fulfilled —" Gentiles shall come to thy light, and kings to the brightness of thy rising." Possibly on this was founded the legend which relates that the Chaldean sages from beyond Euphrates, astrologers who had observed a star in the East, came to the rocky cave to greet the new-born Messiah with costly gifts of gold and spice. The same chronicler also avers that Herod the Great ordered at this time the massacre of all the infants under two years of age in Bethlehem, and that Rabbi Jeshua was only saved by the opportune flight of his parents to Egypt through the Divine interposition of a vision or dream.

Perhaps of all great men such legends exist or have existed, for the natural dramatic instinct of uncivilised chroniclers tends to the elaboration of an introduction worthy the dignity of the subsequent career. But in this case we have the additional motive that the advent of the Messiah had become in Rabbi Jeshua's time a definite dogma, every detail of which had been laboriously worked out by Rabbinic exegesis.

In the chronicle of Rabbi Saul we find a further advance in the process of elaboration. The Jerusalem version is content with the bare statement that Rabbi Jeshua was born at Bethlehem, without any explanation of the fact that the scene of his career was mainly laid in Galilee; but the pupil of Gamaliel attempts to give a reason for the apparent paradox in the statement that Rabbi Jeshua's parents were of the house of David, and came to the town to pay the tax levied by the Romans after the banishment of Archelaus to Vienne.

Unfortunately, however, this theory is vitiated by the anachronism which it entails; for if it be true that Rabbi Jeshua was born in the reign of Herod the Great, as Rabbi Saul himself says, he was already ten years old when the taxation by Cyrenius commenced. Nor is this the only anachronism to be noted in the pages of Rabbi Saul; and it is for such reasons that we must beware of accepting as authoritative the statements of a writer more remarkable for the beauty of his language and the catholicity of his sentiments than for the fidelity of his historical statements concerning his hero.

The Jerusalem version, as we have seen, describes a visit of astrologers and a massacre of infants. It is true that neither event is recorded in the history of Josephus; but it is quite possible that the pilgrimage of a few Chaldean sheikhs may have been thought unworthy of notice, and that the slaughter of the twenty or thirty babes, who would have been under two years of age at any one time in a little village like Bethlehem, may have been forgotten amongst the many murders of the cruel Idumean. It is, however, remarkable that Rabbi Saul omits both these stories, and that, instead of a hurried flight to Egypt, he speaks of the performance in the temple at Jerusalem of the rites of purification, and of the immediate return of Rabbi Jeshua's parents to Galilee.

None of the other existing versions of Rabbi Jeshua's life make any allusions to the legends of his birth and childhood; but among the discordant traditions which are noticed by the Jerusalem chronicle, and that of Rabbi Saul, there is one which, however legendary it may be, deserves a passing notice on account of its poetic beauty.

Rabbi Saul relates that on the night when Rabbi Jeshua was born in the cave stable of the Khan, there were shepherds watching their herds of black goats and fat-tailed sheep on the dreary chalk plateau of Migdol Eder, where, according to the rabbis, the Messiah was first to appear advancing from the great desert beneath, clad in garments dyed red with blood.

In the gloomy caves which here formed the night shelter of the flocks, hedged in with the prickly thorns of the lotos, and crouched round the smouldering fire of mastic shrubs, the rude herdsmen sat among their beasts in the dark and cold. The bitter wind from the sea swept across that barren wold; and in the fitful moonlight the thick flakes of snow might be seen falling silently.

Then, according to the poetic fancy of the writer, a beam of celestial light pierced through the night, and the white forms of the feathered angel-host were seen in the glory of its radiance sailing through the snowstorm and rejoicing in strains which rose above the fury of the gale, while they announced to the terror-stricken hinds the advent of the long expected Messiah. Surely if there were any to whom such message of the birth of Rabbi Jeshua should have been told it was to the poor, the ignorant, the despised peasantry, whom he loved, and among whom he lived and worked.

But in thus enumerating the legends which surround the birth of Rabbi Jeshua we have wandered beyond the sober pale of history, and have deserted the simple story as related by Simeon has Saddik. Of the birth, parentage, and childhood of his master he gives us no account, and of the fabulous and contradictory genealogies which appear in the other chronicles not a trace is found in the earlier narrative.

It is even entirely uncertain to what city Rabbi Jeshua belonged, whether to Nazareth, in the hills of Zebulon, or to Capharnahum, on the borders of the lake of Kinnereth. It is uncertain from what tribe he was descended; and, as will be seen later, there is no good reason to suppose that he belonged to the house of David, which (although the famous Hillel is said to have claimed a descent from David on his mother's side) had probably become extinct even earlier than the Maccabean period; and would have been hunted down by the Idumean kings, had any representatives remained, with the same remorseless cruelty which was shown in the murder of the last surviving members of the princely family of the Hasmoneans.

It seems probable that the father of Rabbi Jeshua was a mechanic, and that he belonged to the small class (whence many other famous rabbis had sprung) of those who, removed by one degree from the abject poverty and ceaseless toil of the ploughman or the goatherd, were yet obliged to support themselves by their simple skill in the craft of carpentry or smith's work, tent-weaving or pottery—the primitive trades of an uncivilized agricultural race.

One scene alone we are able to picture to the mind's eye. It is the interior of a squalid building rudely constructed of stone, with a domed roof and whitewashed walls, a wooden desk or cupboard on one side, and an inscription in Hebrew over the door. From the building as we approach comes the hum of many children's voices, repeating the verses of the sacred Torah in unthinking and perfunctory monotone.

The aged teacher sits silent in the midst. As we look in, we see his huge turban, his grey beard, and solemn features appearing over the ruddy faces of the dark-eyed boys who sit on the floor around him. The long row of tiny red slippers extends along the wall near the door. The earthern water-bottle stands on the mat beside the Khazzan, or synagogue teacher, and in the cool shade of that dingy room the ceaseless murmur of the humble scholars of the village goes forth in the silence of the hot Eastern noon.

They are children of the richer members of the village community: of the Batlanim, or "men of leisure," who form the representative congregation at every synagogue service; of the "standing men," who go up yearly with the village priest for a week to Jerusalem, to fulfil similar functions in the Temple ritual. The poor cowherd may gaze from the door (standing in the scorching sun as his goats wander past) at the cool room with its chattering scholars; but he has no money to pay the Khazzan's fee, and must live and die like his forefathers, ignorant of even the letters of the alphabet.

Alone among this little crowd, we mark the noble and beautiful child, who is hereafter to be Rabban Jeshua -has Saddik. We note how the glorious words of the old Hebrew poets go home to his heart. We know how he ponders over the comments of the teacher, and treasures the assurance that these old prophecies refer not to a long departed and glorious history, but to the great hopes of the future for Israel, to the reign of the Prince Messiah, and the triumph of the faith of Jehovah.

In those dark eyes the fire of genius already burns. In those eager and tremulous features, the enthusiasm of a great nature is already manifest. In the lessons of the village school in Galilee, the foundation of a world-wide fame is laid.

Such was the education of Rabbi Jeshua. To the Jew, the rearing of children was one of the most important of human duties. "By the breath of the school children," says one rabbi, "the world is saved." Even on the Sabbath eve they might be taught, and not for the building of the Temple itself might their education be laid aside.

But what was meant by education? Was it such as we now witness in the West? the inculcation of elementary truths of science and history, arithmetic or art? "At five years," said Judah son of Tamai, "a child should study the Bible, and at ten the Mishna." It is the prototype of the modern Moslem school that we should recognise in the ancient synagogue teaching. It was the study of the sacred Torah which, like the study of the Koran among Moslem children, formed the sum total of education.

The great square letters in which sacred books were written were learned by the infant Jeshua in the Galilean schoolroom. From his rustic master he derived the traditional interpretation of the holy books, against which in the years of his manhood his sense of truth rebelled. With Hillel and Shammai, indeed—the great Jerusalem rabbis—he was unacquainted, nor was he probably ever received into the college which their pupils then taught at the capital. The originality of his genius was not warped by the narrow Pharisaic spirit; but the bent of his mind was nevertheless directed by those days in the dark synagogue school towards that intent study of the Law of Moses, through which he became at length a master in Israel.

Thus, ignorant of such science as the world then knew, unacquainted alike with the mystic philosophy of Egypt or Asia Minor, with the discoveries of heathen students, with the history of foreign lands, Rabbi Jeshua's ardent and poetic nature developed year by year under the influence of a religious training. The Songs of David became precious to him; the parables which surrounded him by sea and land were read by the eyes of inborn genius; the hopes of the chosen race became the desires of his heart. Unknown and unheeded by the goatherds and cowherds, the fishers and craftsmen, the dull rabbis and the fanatic Pharisees, the growth of a master-mind went on in their midst.

With early manhood came that other influence already noticed—the preaching of Hanan, the hermit of Bethania. Already, no doubt, the hypocrisies of orthodoxy, the man-made dogmas of rabbinical commentators, the specious evasions of the plain meaning of the Law, the disingenuous explanations of ungrateful facts, had disgusted the truth-seeking student with the constituted creed of the land.

To Hanan, then, he turned as a guide and a master. In him he found the earnestness, the enthusiasm, the austere and fanatic self-devotion which could satisfy his nature; and to the sect of the Hasaya he became attached so soon as he had received from the hermit's hand the initiatory rite of ablution.

From the river banks and the crowds of listeners, he fled at first to the solitude of the desert. He sought, as Elijah of old, the retreat where he might brood undisturbed over the thoughts which strove within him. How long his hermit life endured Rabbi Simeon does not tell us; but we know at least that he only returned to Galilee after the death of Hanan, and it is probable therefore that the forty days to which other chroniclers confine his stay in the wilderness owe their origin rather to an attempted parallelism between Rabbi Jeshua and his forerunner Elijah, than to any source of actual information.

Of the hermit life of Rabbi Jeshua after his conversion to the Hasaya tenets, Simeon, the chronicler, speaks with awe. The dreary wastes round the Bitter Sea, the marl hills with their salt streams, the red cliffs with their caverns, the ghastly and fantastic chalk-peaks, the tangled jungle of Jordan, constituted a region of dreadful solitude commonly believed to be haunted by unclean spirits. Here, fed by the lotus fruit, the locusts, or the wild bees, the solitary rabbi wandered. Later chroniclers have claimed to know the various details of weird temptations which beset him, and have elaborated out of the narrative of Simeon has Saddik a legendary history of a rabbinical contest between Jeshua and the fiend. They quote, however, no authority for their account of these wonderful facts; and when we remember the immense development of supernatural machinery in their narratives as contrasted with that of Simeon, we are led to suspect the addition of marvellous embellishments, such as Oriental writers appear to consider not beyond the legitimate licence of an elegant historian, just as some artists allow themselves the use of fancy foregrounds to actual scenes.

The answer to our first question remains therefore almost a negative. Who was Rabbi Jeshua? What were his parents, his descent, his tribe, his home? What were the facts of his desert life, the thoughts which grew up in his mind in solitude? The answer must still be, that we do not know. If we would avoid the charge of diluting history with fanciful illustration, and of accepting with equal credulity the legends of later chroniclers and the superstitions of the original biography, we must be content to record the simple facts that a Jewish child grew up in Galilee to manhood, and retreated from men to a hermit life in the wilderness. For there are probably few in the nineteenth century who would think themselves justified in adding to such an account the quaint conceit of Rabbi Simeon's narrative that "he was in the wilderness tempted of Satan, and was with the wild beasts, and the angels ministered to him."

CHAPTER III.

SOCIETY IN THE TETRARCHIES.

The Procurator of Judea—Roman rule in Syria—Imitation of Roman civilisation by the Herodians—Life in Jerusalem—Political parties—Hillel and Shammai — Jewish metaphysics — Scientific ignorance—Cynicism—A student's life—The peasantry—Superstition—Ideas of the future—The national expectation.

How invaluable to the student of Jewish history would be the memoirs of a Roman procurator at Jerusalem in the first century of our era. How fresh would be the light which might be thrown on the society of the times by the comments of an educated and refined heathen charged with the task of governing an almost ungovernable people.

We may picture to ourselves the astonishment with which a statesman accustomed to the simple policy of "Panem et Circenses" would regard the outburst of fanaticism roused by his attempts to gain popularity. He finds the leaven of the heathen regarded with abhorrence, and the games of the circus treated as degrading exhibitions. Even the attempt to supply the city with fresh water through a well-made aqueduct leads to a riot. The populace refuse to be awed, to be coaxed, or even to be amused.

How squalid and ugly the Holy City itself must have appeared to the Italian fresh from the glories of imperial Rome. How he must have missed the fair gardens, the public baths, and the great river; and what could there be to interest the fellow-countrymen of Horace and Virgil in the eager speculations of the rabbis on the permissibility of wearing a wooden leg on the Sabbath?

The absence of any æsthetic feeling in the architecture of the city, or in the rude native manufactures, must have been equally at variance with the elegant taste of the Italian. Had not the Golden Eagle—a solitary ornament to the immense Temple façade—been recently hacked to pieces by fanatic priests? What could compensate in the "sordid and absurd" rites of the sanctuary for the gay processions of flower-crowned youths and maidens, for the wondrous beauty of the statues, for the pomp and enjoyment of an Italian feast-day? How lugubrious in his ears must the blast of the great goat-horns and the monotonous beat of the tabors have sounded. How hateful in time must the immutable solemnity and fanatical abhorrence, which manifested themselves in every face his look encountered, have become to the cultivated and refined patrician condemned to the exile of a Syrian capital.

Among all their subjects there were perhaps none whom the great Roman race found harder to rule or more difficult to understand than the Jews. The power of self-adaptation was perhaps not less a cause of Roman success than the hardy courage by which they first won their empire. The wise tolerance through which Alexander subdued so many different races became a maxim of the statecraft of the shrewd Italian nation, and the rule of the Romans was preferred by the Jews to the tyranny of the Idumean kings. But in the Hebrews the Latins found a people so utterly intolerant of every creed save their own as to be deaf to every suggestion of a common belief veiled by variety of symbols, and yet possessing so fierce an intensity of character, so complete a conviction, so absolute an individuality, as to render it impossible that their conquerors should ignore the faith of their subjects or substitute the ritual of Jove for the rites of Jehovah.

"All things," says the Roman historian, "are with them profane which are with us sacred; and again, those practices are allowed among them which are by us esteemed most abominable." "The Jews," he adds, "have no conception of more than one divine being. Among themselves there is an ever ready and unchanging fidelity and kindness, but bitter enmity to all others."

Not that the great Italians were incapable of appreciating all that was noble and poetic in the faith of the Hebrews. In the Augustan age the poetry of the Jews found its way to the capital of the world, and in Virgil's Eclogues we are astonished to recognise the influence of Messianic literature. The Alexandrine poem written in Greek, and recording, under the guise of prophecy, the events of the great struggles preceding the establishment of the Empire, and concluding with the epical description of the reign of Messiah, was read, admired, and paraphrased by the learned dilettanti of Italy; and in the Sibylline books we recognise the reflex action of the East on the West, the influence of the Hebrew on his Roman master.

Yet, though the race-pride of the self-chosen people estranged them from their conquerors, who for their part regarded them with mingled contempt and astonishment, the wise rule of the Romans rendered them more acceptable to the

Jewish nation than were the Idumean monarchs, who professed to be worshippers of Jehovah.

When the great tyrant died at Jericho, and Augustus decided the quarrels of his heirs by carving his dominions into four small provinces, the first petition preferred by the Jews, and again reiterated until finally granted, was not the recognition of a native prince, but the union of the Judean tetrarchy with the exclusively Roman province of Coele Syria.

From the time of the wise Maccabeus onwards the Jews had indeed been accustomed to regard Rome as the safest ally for the holy nation; and, with exception of the short episode of the violent and unwise tyranny of Pontius Pilate, which endured only ten years, the rule of the procurators for half a century appears to have secured for the country a greater degree of peace and prosperity than it had ever boasted since the death of Simon the Hasmonean.

It is not easy to grasp at first the idea of that half-civilised society which must in the East have resulted from a provincial imitation of the manners of the Roman capital. Yet we have abundant evidence that some such copy of pagan society was presented by the little court of Antipas not less than by that of his father Herod. In the Alexandria or Beirût of to-day we may perhaps contemplate a similar reflex of Western civilisation influencing an Oriental people. We find the fashions, the customs, the vices of Europe caricatured as it were among the more worthless and dissipated of the rising generation in the Levant. We find cheap reproductions of Western manufactures, tawdry imitations of Western luxuries, absurd exaggerations of Western customs, feeble reproductions of Western art and thought. The imitation lacks the vigour, the individuality, and the beauty of the original; and the absence of that spirit of humour which distinguishes the European from the Asiatic, converts the polished product of Aryan development into a ludicrously solemn and childishly feeble travesty.

Such no doubt was the result of an attempt at the reproduction of Roman civilisation by the semi-pagan Idumean monarchs. The country had been impoverished by the imposts laid on the Jews for the adornment of the coast cities inhabited by pagans: yet how poor appear these boasted works compared with the great productions of Italian genius. How barbarous and debased is the semi-classic style of the imperfectly carved cornices which still appear above the porches of the rock-cut tombs of Judea, belonging to this vaunted period of a superficial prosperity.

In Jerusalem it is true that a theatre and a hippodrome were erected by the Herods; and Arab robbers may perhaps have been occasionally condemned to fight for their lives with panthers from Jordan, or with a few hyenas from the mountains. But where were to be found the enthusiastic masses which thronged the great amphitheatres of Italy, and whose fierce delight rendered the meaning of such a spectacle comprehensible? A trembling crowd without, a few dissipated youths within, a spirit of undying hatred roused by an exhibition of remorseless cruelty, were all that could be expected in the Holy City.

Such we may perhaps imagine was the pagan aspect of Syrian society:—a Roman procurator despising his subjects, and lamenting his exile from the pleasures and luxuries of Rome; an Idumean court, feebly aping the manners and the arts of the West, hated by the nation and despised by the conquerors; a half-hearted attempt to reform the immutable East after the contemporary fashion of the ever-changing West.

But what in the eyes of the people itself was the condition of the country and of the race? "He who has not seen Jerusalem," said a rabbi who perhaps never travelled more than a sabbath day's journey beyond its walls, "has never seen a beautiful city." Entering within its tower-crowned walls the Jew passed with awe the palace-gardens where thousands of doves circled among the trees, and where it was whispered that brazen idols of the heathen ran with water as cool fountains among the groves. Here in the narrow shady street the money-changers sat before their piles of silver. Here among camels and asses, heaps of fruit and vegetables, the solemn rabbis jostled the sun-brown peasant crowds which chattered over their produce in the glaring dusty market-place. Here was the very window of the college where the great Hillel was found frozen and snow-covered, listening as a youth to the teaching of the rabbis whose instruction he was too poor to pay for, yet of whom only five years later he became the prince and leader. Here again bloomed the one rose-garden which remained from the time of the Prophets. Here on all sides rose the palaces of priests and princes, the wondrous bridge, the mighty ramparts of the Temple.

Down the roughly paved lane, through the cool fruit market, over the bridge, the pilgrim passed to the Holy House, and through the great cloisters, whose gigantic columns stood half-built round the broad and rocky platform. Here in their booths sat the money-changers and the sellers of sacrifices.

In the centre rose the huge fane glittering with barbaric gold; while on the oaken trellice above the mystic veil the great bunches of golden grapes, each six feet high, hung by their hooks from the golden vine stem.

Passing by the stone piers, with inscriptions in an unknown tongue which warned the accursed heathen to remain at a fitting distance, the devout Jew entered the inner enclosure. Here in the galleries sat his veiled fellow country-women; while on the floor of the court, in the glare of the great candlesticks, goodly youths danced in the cool of the starry night, with torches in their hands, singing the psalm of the feast-day. Or in the day-time the rabbis famous from Dan to Beersheba might be seen, sitting on the steps of the court, teaching their disciples; the lepers might be watched as they came up to stick a thumb and a toe through the brazen gate to the priest who purified them from within. The blast of the goat-horns summoned the congregation to the sacrifice. The rude pile of stone and pebbles, gleaming with whitewash and streaming with blood, smoked with the three columns of its pine-wood fires. The lowing of oxen and the bleating of flocks mingled with the chant of the Levites, as the golden vessels were borne up the steps of the Holy House, and the priests disappeared behind the veil into the solemn shadow of the unapproachable sanctuary.

How unfamiliar to most of us are the scenes of that ancient life in Jerusalem. Can we picture the sadness of the autumn fast for rain when in the sultry mid-day, beneath a heaven grey with the east wind, the arks were brought out of the synagogues into the market-place and strewn with ashes? Or the joy of the people when the stormy downpour flooded the streets and threatened to submerge the "Stone of Proclamation" itself? Can we realise the hospitality which provided a free table for strangers at the door of every house in Jerusalem, or see in imagination the search by candlelight for leaven in every room or cellar before the Passover —the yearly dances of the maidens with willow branches, the yearly procession of baskets with the firstfruits, the dismissal of the black goat to the desert mountain down which he was dashed, or the booths which rose on the housetops at the autumn feast?

From such hints of a condition of life which has no modern counterpart we might gather the outward aspect of the Holy City, the capital of the country, and the centre to which the devout multitude continually gravitated. But as Jerusalem with its sanctuary contrasted with the mud hamlets of the surrounding land, forming the ideal of beauty and splendour to the simple people to whom the capitals of the world were unknown, so did the city life contrast with that of the rural peasant population. A marked line separated the rich from the poor—the priest or rabbi from the "people of the land," the student from the rustic. No middle class of merchants, traders, or bourgeois existed, no link between the two ranks of society; and the broad distinction thus remarkable had an influence on the history of Rabbi Jeshua which renders it of peculiar interest for the purpose of the present inquiry.

Let us consider first the life of the upper class of the Jewish nation. Politically, they were divided into three parties at the capital, and from a religious point of view into two. There was the great popular party, whose hope lay in the expectation of a national future, which had ceased for more than a century to be better than a dream. There was the Herodian faction, which schemed and plotted for the restoration of Archelaus. There was the rich and powerful party which, led by the great priestly family of Hanan, supported the existing authority of the Roman procurator. The Pharisees, who were ever the leaders of the multitude, formed the mainstay of the national party, and united with the Herodians in the common object of expelling the Romans from the Holy Land. The Sadducees, whose materialistic indifference to the future was consistent only with the enjoyment of temporal prosperity, supported the great priestly family which belonged to their sect. Of the Zealots, whose unconquerable aversion to all human rulers led half a century later to the great national catastrophe, few ventured then to show their faces so near to the seat of Roman government; while the humble and submissive character of the Hasaya, though rendering them less obnoxious as a sect to the ruling power, led to their retreat from mankind into the desert, and made the appearance of the white robe of the order a rare occurrence in the streets of Jerusalem.

Shut out from power, and from the duties of the Pontificate, the Pharisees had abundant leisure for the one study known to the Jew—the interpretation of the Law of Moses. It was little more than half a century since the famous Hillel had come from Babylonia to Jerusalem. By descent a Benjamite, and on his mother's side claiming to trace back to the house of David, he was educated by Shemaiah and Abtalyon, and manifested in a few years his superiority to all their other disciples in the treatment of the delicate question whether the Paschal lamb might be slain on the Sabbath. For twenty years he held the position of Prince of the Sanhedrim, and died only a few years before Rabbi Jeshua was born.

With Hillel commenced the systematic study of the written and of the traditional Law. The disputations between his school and that of his contentious disciple, Shammai, led to so minute a definition of many precepts, that the metaphysical subtlety of the difference renders it almost invisible to the blunt Western mind; but however bitter the controversies of the Beth-Din might be, they passed unnoticed by the rulers of the land, for the wise counsel of their master was followed by Hillel and Shammai alike, "Love thy work, hate dominion, and be unknown to Government."

The love of grappling with abstruse metaphysical problems, and the habit of attaching to them an importance transcending that of more practical questions of life and morals, appears to be distinctive of the Semitic mind.

Amongst the Syrian Christians of the early ages of the Church first arose those subtle but fierce controversies which make up the history of the Christian heresies. Among the learned doctors of our own day, the subtleties of the Koran are in like manner discussed. Based on the acceptation of certain documents as written through divine inspiration, these great schools alike recognise the possibility that the sound, the position, the choice of every word and letter of the divine commands, may have a hidden meaning which it is incumbent on the believer to search out.

Heresy had long since ceased to spread in the Holy Land in the days of Hillel. The Samaritans, it is true, remained impenitent in worshipping at Gerizim, and in awaiting a Messiah, son of Ephraim; but the fatal error of the Egyptians had been purged from the land. No teacher in Jerusalem sought any longer to explain away the history of Israel and the commands of the law as allegorical and symbolic. The doctrines of the Incarnate Word, of the old Adam, of the Angel of the Presence, the mysteries of the Cabbala, and the engrafting of heathen philosophy on Jewish orthodoxy were heresies confined to the renegades of Alexandria. The attention of the pious was concentrated on the right understanding of the Law, and on the building up of "hedges" to render transgression impossible. Freedom of conscience, security from persecution, and the purification of the nation from heresy, gave leisure for the settlement of such important questions as that of the lawfulness of eating an egg which was known to have been laid on the Sabbath.

If the Jews were right in their fundamental doctrine, such discussion was the logical outcome of sincere desire to obey the divine command. If it were true that the law of Moses contained the sum total of possible and necessary truth for man, then we should do wrong to underrate the importance of those questions which rabbinical authorities raised and solved.

But if we must believe in the growth of the mind of man, in the right of the free genius of a nation to shake off the trammels of an earlier faith, and of laws made for a long defunct condition of civilisation, the self-torture of the conscientious Jew must appear to our eyes a miserable diversion of energy and intellectual power from noble ends.

The study of the Law formed the sum total of education. Man was as yet unconscious of the great lessons which might be learned in the contemplation of the "wonderful works of God." That by the accumulated experience and observation of generations great secrets might be laid bare, great principles evolved for the practical benefit of the race and for the development of human power, were facts which had scarcely presented themselves to the minds of the nations then furthest advanced in knowledge : facts to which the Jew in the self-conceit of ignorance was supremely indifferent.

If, for instance, we think of medicine as the most necessary of the sciences, how absolutely was any knowledge of the art unknown to the Jew. Herod's doctors immersed the diseased monarch in a vessel of warm oil as a cure for his complicated maladies. For palsy, rheumatism, and nervous pain, the Jew then as in our own times bathed in the intermittent pool which rises in the Kedron valley, or travelled to the baths of Callirrhoe or Tiberias. For tooth-ache he carried pepper in his mouth, for ear-ache the egg of a locust was a cure, for sleeplessness the tooth of a living fox, for hydrophobia the skin of a male adder, for ague the nails from the cross of a malefactor.

In spite of the long captivity in Babylon, the Jews never learned the science of astronomy which their captors had prosecuted since the days of Abraham. They still watched the new moon for the calculation of their months; they still condemned to eternal punishment the man who studied Greek philosophy.

Had such devotion to the study of the Law been accompanied by any remarkable moral elevation of character, the prejudice against other and more useful subjects of research might have been pardonable; but such evidence as we have goes rather to prove that the immorality of the great Greek age was purer than the organised and permitted uncleanliness of the devout Jew. The narrow jealousies, the insane conceit, the cynical scepticism of rabbinical teachers must be contrasted with the rude nobility of the Northern nations whose pretensions to holiness were so much less arrogant. "There is no blessing," says the Mishna, "at food, for women, slaves, and children." "Whoever converses much with women," says Rabbi Joseh, "brings evil on himself, neglects the study of the Law, and will at last inherit hell." With such an estimate of the influence and purity of their helpmates, what wonder if Jews were allowed by law to divorce one woman if another was more pleasing in their eyes.

Self-concentrated and self-content, the student of the Law was enjoined to pass his life in the contemplation of his own salvation. He was, in the words of the Mishna, to pursue his research, "with study, diligence, and eloquence; with an understanding and intelligent heart, with dread and meekness, fear and joy, with attendance on the wise, with the aid of his companions, through disputation with disciples, with soberness, with study of the Torah and of the Mishna, in purity with little sleep, with little talk, with little work, little sport, little pleasure, and little intercourse with the world; with slowness to anger, a good heart, confidence in the wise, and patience in chastisement, knowing his station, and rejoicing in his lot." Such is the character of the Jewish student, as sketched by the masters under whom he learned.

But what of those who had no leisure for such study, who could not leave their fields and their flocks, who could not pay the fee which admitted them to the college? Was there any provision for teaching to them the lessons of righteousness and of morality to be found in the Law, or any communion between the pious and the poor?

"No boor," said Rabbi Gamaliel, "can be fearful of sin; nor can a peasant be a saint; neither will he who is engaged in traffic become wise." Those who knew not the Law were no better than the beasts that perish; yet we find no saying of the wise which inculcates the teaching of the poor, or the instruction of the ignorant peasant. It was thus that the broad line of separation between class and class was drawn, and it was in this lack of sympathy that the real weakness of the nation consisted.

In every town there was a synagogue; to every

synagogue a school was attached. From each town a representative congregation accompanied the order of the priests in due turn to Jerusalem. But these were the duties and privileges of the rich and the learned, of those who knew the Law. Piety and good breeding go together in the East, and the poor are as little concerned with one as with the other.

We thus become aware that the religion of Jerusalem was not the faith of the mass of the common people. Only forty-two thousand Jews returned with Ezra from captivity, and we may well doubt if the majority of the nation in the days when the country was so thickly populated were Jews at all. Their tongue was that of the Canaanite, their worship was that of the high places; and, save through the medium of a translation, the scriptures were unintelligible to the peasantry. The altars of local deities still stood (and still stand) on the mountain tops in Palestine; the shady trees and groves of the aboriginal cultus were still preserved; the stone heaps of Mercury were still built up, the mourning for Tammuz still annually observed in Bethlehem. Thus by religion, by language, and by race, the peasant was separated irrevocably from the richer student in the city.

Taxed by the Roman and by the priest, oppressed by the soldiery, despised by his fellows, the poor tiller of the soil spent his days in a ceaseless round of toil, uncheered by the prospect of any brighter future in this world. In the miserable hamlets of the plains, fever and dysentery, cholera and spleen swept off their victims year by year, and none were found to minister to the poor, or to alleviate their sufferings by counsel and compassion. The practice of a charity which even now, as of old, pauperises half the nation was the nearest approach to philanthropy known to the Jew; but the broad principles of the Mishna manifest the want of sympathy between great and small, when they lay down that all ass-drivers are wicked, all camel-drivers honest, all pigeon-fanciers liars, and all physicians destined for hell.

Yet over the poor and ignorant, the doctrines of the Pharisee held an important influence. The love of wonder is innate in the mind of the untaught, and the marvels which the teachers of the people described sunk deep into the hearts of the unhappy. There was going to be a new earth, a new Jerusalem, a new age of glory and triumph. The miseries of the faithful were to be compensated by long life, plentiful harvests and vintages, innumerable wives and children. The great feast was to be some day spread on the mountains, and the judgment of the heathen to be pronounced.

Meantime, beneath the earth in the gloomy caverns of Sheol the souls of just and unjust awaited the immediate future. In Abraham's bosom slept the faithful and elect; in the burning lake the wicked writhed in hopeless expectation of a similar but eternal future. And, mingled with such hopes and such fears, the old superstitions still flourished: the queen of heaven was still honoured in the wild districts of the hills, and the children still passed through the fire to Moloch in the obscure and outlying villages.

This, then, if we have read aright the scattered indications of contemporary history, was the condition of the land when the career of Rabbi Jeshua opened. The power of Rome was established peacefully, but the civilisation of the West had failed to influence the mass of the nation in the Syrian province. The feeble reflex of that civilisation might be found in the tone and manners of the Idumean court; but the thoughts and actions of the nation were more deeply influenced by the priestly caste at Jerusalem. In the far mountains of Galilee the germ of future rebellion was growing up among the turbulent Zealots. In the deserts of Jordan the monastic spirit developed among the Hasaya and the Abionim. The people of the land toiled uncared for and unpitied. Yet there was one passionate longing which still united the nation, and it is to this hope of the people that our attention must now for a moment be directed.

CHAPTER IV.

THE HOPE OF THE PEOPLE.

Sleeping champions—The origin of the idea—Types—The return of Elijah—The heir to David—His character—Birth pangs of the Messiah—The Gentiles—The new earth—Dante's prototype—Later views as to the Messiah.

IN the dark vault at Kronenburg, with his arm beneath his head, clad in iron and steel, and his great beard grown through the table, sleeps Holger Danske, waiting the day of Denmark's greatest need.

In the enchanted island of Avilion, where never wind blows loudly, rests the wounded Arthur, whose return England no longer expects.

In the hall of his palace Frederic the Red Beard awaits likewise the call of his country. In Russia it is Ivan the Terrible who will return to chastise the boyar and help the serf. In Islam it is the twelfth Imâm.

In Judah it was, and is, the Messiah.

What is the meaning of this constant tradition among races so distinct in character and feelings? and what is the lesson that may thence be drawn?

The lesson is this, that however much we may write or speak of the "people" and the "nation," it is by the great men of the nation that its history is made, and in the heroes of the people that the hope of the future is found.

To all of us the present seems to be the worst time. The future is full of hopes, the trials of the past are half forgotten. We stand on a stony and thorny foreground, we look back or forwards to a distant scene whose harsher features are blended by the intervening haze. The thorns and the stones are as many in the distance as are those beneath our feet; but they are no longer seen, and only the grander features of the distant landscape are visible to our eyes.

Such also is the national memory of a glorious history, the popular hope for a more glorious future. It is the return of the past that is eagerly longed for—the reappearance of the great men whose greatness was perhaps recognized only after death. Woe to the nation which has no such dreams of the future and no such discontent with the actual present!

The expectation of an awakened champion must

in past times, when men really believed in and hoped for such things, have been most vivid and earnest in times of national depression and trouble. Thus it was with the Jews. Tacitus tells of a time when they were ruled by native kings, "because the Macedonians had become weak, and the Parthians were not yet very powerful, and the Romans were very remote." Yet this great opportunity passed away without profit to the chosen people. The Hasmonean power was lost in the corruption of that great house, the strength of the nation was dissipated by the quarrels of its factions, the chance of attaining a position of political importance in Western Asia was for ever lost.

It was at this time that the idea of an Anointed Prince first developed among the disappointed patriots of Jerusalem. If we look earlier in their history we find no such hope expressed; if we glance lower down the page the idea rapidly gains in intensity and importance.

When Judas Maccabeus rose as a sledge-hammer to break down the bondage of the Seleucidæ, he laid no claim to the office of Messiah. His brethren were consecrated as princes and priests until a faithful prophet should arise to direct the destinies of the nation; and the honesty of purpose and of thought among the simple patriots whose valour saved the Jewish faith from extinction is evidenced by the fact that no fictitious claims to prophetic power were advanced by them.

We have perhaps but a vague idea of the views which were common among the Jews on the subject of the Messiah. To us the word implies an expected supernatural monarch whose advent is yet awaited by the chosen people. Yet there were many Messiahs, past and future, among the Jews. The high priest was a Messiah, "anointed" with the holy oil which consecrated Aaron. The priest who went out to battle was the Messiah for war. The king was the Messiah-Neged, or anointed chief. In the Targums we have two future Messiahs predicted—the son of Judah, and the son of Ephraim. Among all these it is to the expectation of a future King of the house of David that we are accustomed to confine the meaning of the term Messiah.

Correct ideas of the Jewish expectation of such a future prince may be derived from the early Apocalyptic literature, from the Talmud and from the Targums, rather than from the passages in the Scriptures which form the text of these extended commentaries. The Book of Enoch, the third Sibylline book, the fourth of Ezra, the Psalms of Solomon, belong to the period under consideration, and in these we find the idea of the future King gradually developed. In the Targums we trace the subtle casuistry whereby the great theory was elaborated from original utterances having apparently no connection with the subject. In the Bible we find only Cyrus called Messiah, in the Targums we count no less than seventy passages where the word and the idea are interpolated.

At the basis of the whole of this wonderful structure of passionate hope and faith, lies the idea of a hidden and more elevated meaning, to be attributed to the words of writers to whom perhaps no such idea was ever present. It is the same tendency which has converted the touching and simple stories of the Iliad into great myths of the aspirations of the soul, and of the phenomena of nature. It was in the same spirit that Philo explained away the history of Moses. It is in the same spirit that we apply the denunciations of Gog and Magog to the Russian devastators of our own days.

Once admit that the words written may have a meaning other than that which meets the eye, and this extension of ancient prophecies, this amplification of ancient poetry into a forecast of a great future, may be carried on century after century for an unending duration. Once create the idea of a "type," and the final facts typified will change as generation succeeds generation.

Is it not thus that from the poetic declamations of the Hebrew prophets the idea of the future King was evolved? On what authority does the Targum see typified in the Exodus the going forth of Messiah from Rome? For what reason should the blessings invoked on Cyrus be transferred to a future prince? Have we not also in our own times seen the names of Antichrist and the beast applied, in one generation to Napoleon Bonaparte, and in the next, with equal certainty, to Napoleon III.? Nay, what great ruler from the time of Julian downwards escaped this imputation, if he once placed himself in conflict with the Church? It is from the Jews that this habit of referring the poetry of the past to the hope of the immediate future has been derived: it is on the fanciful extension of the scope of ancient aspirations that the whole theory of a Messiah rests. It is in the same spirit that Josephus sees the prophecies of Daniel twice fulfilled, once in the desolation caused by Antiochus Epiphanes, and again in the final destruction of Jerusalem by the Romans.

The earliest orthodox idea of a future leader seems to have been that of a prophet rather than a king. It is to such a belief that the writer of the

Book of Maccabees so often refers, and we at once discern a foundation for such an expectation in the promise of a prophet "like unto" Moses, which is still devoutly believed by the Samaritans at Shechem.

In the book of Malachi, the contemporary of Nehemiah, closing the prophetic canon of the Jewish Scriptures, we find this expectation developed into the idea of the return of Elijah, preceding the impending day of judgment; and such a belief once implanted in the Jewish mind could never again be rooted out.

But with the decadence of the great Hasmonean house, the hope of the future began to centre chiefly round the restoration of the family of David to the throne of Israel.

There was no difficulty in finding allusions to the restored glories of the ancient royal family in the books of the earlier prophets; and when once the pious students who led the thought of the day had convinced themselves that these passages referred not to the past, but to the future, the promises therein contained became the definite and immediate hope of the nation.

The King Messiah then was to be an actual and earthly monarch, born at Bethlehem of Judah, of the lineage of David, and reigning in Jerusalem

The earlier expectation of a coming prophet was reconciled with this newly-born hope, through the explanation that Elijah should precede the King as a forerunner. Some who held that the resurrection preceded the reign of Messiah believed that the prophet should first return to raise the dead, and should subsequently anoint the awaited prince. Others said that Moses also should be reincarnate, and attend the Messiah at his coming. Others again believed, as do the modern Samaritans, that the Anointed One would remain concealed and unknown among men for a season, before his manifestation.

The portrait of the expected Monarch, as drawn in the so-called Psalms of Solomon, expresses the conception, at the time of our history, of the future hope of Israel.

"A righteous King, Son of David, taught by God, and anointed by Jehovah! He will not place his trust in his horse or his bow, nor multiply silver or gold for war, for his hope is in God, and he shall smite the earth with the word of his mouth. Pure from sin, strong in the Holy Spirit, wise in counsel and great in righteousness, mighty in the fear of God, he shall feed the Lord's flock in faith and truth and lead them to holiness. This is the beauty of the King of Israel! his words are as the words of the just in the midst of an holy people."

There was nothing superhuman in the character of the Prince thus awaited, nothing supernatural in the expected revelation of the heir to David. His reign was to be that of an earthly monarch, his kingdom that of Solomon in his glory. That he should rule the whole earth might appear easily credible to those who knew so little how far beyond the limits of Dan and Beersheba the world extended. The more transcendental of the doctors who discussed the subject, did indeed suppose that the destruction of Jerusalem, and probably the renovation of the world, would precede the coming of Messiah; but the new heavens and the new earth were to be but glorified repetitions of the former, and the new Jerusalem a city of real stones founded on the actual hills of the same mountain region. The spiritual conception of a heavenly city built of jewels and floating above the earth; of a paradise inhabited by angels, and of a fiery Gehenna, belonged to mystic schools of Alexandria rather than to the teaching of the rabbis of Jerusalem before the destruction of the city by the Romans.

A period of trouble was commonly expected to precede the glorious reign of the future King, "the birth pangs of the Messiah," as the Talmud calls it. "In the footprints of the Anointed," says the

Mishna, "impudence shall increase, and there shall be scarcity. The vine shall give fruit, but wine shall be dear; the dominion shall be given to heretics, and there shall be no reproof. The wisdom of the scribes shall stink, and those who fear sin shall be despised, and truth shall fail. Boys shall make the face of the old men pale, the ancient shall rise up before the young. The son shall evil entreat his father, the daughter shall rise up against her mother, and the daughter-in-law against her mother-in-law, and a man's foes shall be they of his own household. The face of that generation shall be as the face of a dog. In whom then shall we trust? In our Father which is in heaven." War, famine, earthquake, anarchy, and corruption must precede the final glory of the revealed Messiah—such is the burden of each book which recounts the expectancy of the century that elapsed before the destruction of the Holy City.

The time of the coming of Messiah was not definitely fixed by Jewish writers. The seventy years of Jeremiah's prophecy, and the seven times seventy of Daniel passed by, and still he came not. The pious ceased to count the years, and fell back on the hope that penitence and prayer might hasten his advent. "Three things," said Rabbi

Zera, "come unexpectedly—the Messiah, a treasure find, and a scorpion!" For the sins of Israel the Messiah was concealed, and some teachers even ventured to say that if Israel did not repent the Messiah might never come at all.

The gathering of foreign foes round the Faithful, and the destruction of the Holy City were expected, as signs of the end, long before Jerusalem was laid low by the Romans. The memory of the cruel devastations of Zion by the Seleucidæ, and the announcement that "the Prince that shall come shall destroy the city and the sanctuary, and the end thereof shall be with a flood," were no doubt the parent ideas of this expectation of a time of trouble for the righteous. The poetic account of an invasion of Syria by the peoples of Asia Minor and Armenia, with the Scythians, the Persians, and the Egyptians as allies, was in like manner transferred to an uncertain future, and formed the foundation of the rabbinical fables of the defeat of Gog and Magog by the Messiah. But the most beautiful of the descriptions of this great battle of the future is perhaps that to be found in the third Sibylline book, written about two centuries before the destruction of Jerusalem by Titus.

"The fruitful earth shall be shaken in those days," says the Sibyl, "by the eternal hand; the fish of the sea, the beasts of the earth, the innumerable tribes of fowl, and all the souls of men, shall quake with dread before the everlasting face, and fear shall be upon them. He shall break the high peaks, the tops of great mountains; and dark night shall be upon all. And the cloudy valleys in the high hills shall be full of the dead, and the rocks shall run with blood, and the stream shall flow to the plain—and the earth shall drink the blood of the slain, and the wild beasts shall feast on their flesh."

To such troubles the reign of Messiah formed the bright contrast which was to follow. The tribes of Israel should be gathered in; the city should be rebuilt; peace, truth, happiness, and prosperity would follow the rule of the righteous King.

But even here a difference of opinion arose among the doctors as to the fate of the Gentiles. The gentle Hillel looked forward to their conversion, and submission to the great Monarch ruling in Jerusalem. The fierce Shammai condemned the enemies of the nation, and all who were not of the chosen race, to death and final annihilation. Perhaps on the whole the balance of opinion was, however, in favour of the belief that until the time of the final judgment the Gentiles, subjected and converted, might be allowed to share in the felicity of the kingdom as servants and serfs of the Jews. "Strangers shall stand and feed your flocks, and the sons of the alien shall be your plowmen and vine-dressers," says the prophet. Of the glories of the future time of peace the Sibyl, no less than the latest rabbinic writers, gives an enthusiastic account:

"The fruitful earth shall give to men in great store the choicest harvest of corn and wine and oil; and from heaven shall drop honey, and fountains of milk shall spring forth. And the city and the field shall be full of good things; and there shall be no more war nor drought upon the earth, nor famine, nor hail to spoil the fruits."

It was not indeed commonly believed that this peaceful reign should endure for ever. The Messiah was mortal, and, with few exceptions, the doctors agreed that his advent would precede the great judgment day, which was to terminate the earth's history after a period of five thousand years from Adam.

Perhaps among the works of poetic genius there is none which we regard as more original and daring in conception than the divine drama of Dante; yet, as there is nothing new under the sun, so in the vision of Enoch, composed by a Jewish poet a century and a half before the fall of Jerusalem, we find the very prototype of that great epic of Christian Italy. The imagery of gloomy mountain chains, of luxuriant meadows, of fiery lakes, of angel guides to the mortal pilgrim, find an origin in the Jewish epic. It is true that a distinctive Jewish tone pervades the Book of Enoch, and that the Italian genius created a gigantic Satan who has no prototype in the Gehenna of the original; but, with this exception, the imagination of the chosen people is responsible for that stupendous fabric of fear and of hope which Christianity inherits.

Such was the great catastrophe of the expected future; but it is important to note that the reign of Messiah was to precede the judgment-day, for in this lies the distinction between the doctrine of the earlier centuries and the more transcendental teaching of later ages, when the kingdom was pictured as a spiritual reign of immortal saints in a heavenly Jerusalem. With the views of this later school, as exemplified in Jewish writings of the early Christian centuries, we are not now concerned. The grotesque exaggerations of the Gemara, the allegories of Philo, the fables of the Cabbalists, may tempt the student by their quaint fancies and poetic conceptions; but if we confine ourselves to the consideration of the original idea of the Kingdom of Messiah as expressed in the Jewish literature of the Herodian ages, we find ourselves in contemplation of a far more material and practical expectation—of the ardent hope for the restoration of the national monarchy, and for the triumphant vindication of the truth of the Jewish faith in the sight of the Gentiles.

That Messiah when he came should be rejected by the nation was an idea so at variance with the very nature of their conception of the future which was immediately expected as to be practically an impossibility to the devout Jew. That a resurrection must precede the foundation of his kingdom was a view equally incompatible with the absence of any ideas of a supernatural character attributable to the expected Monarch.

It is not to our purpose to inquire how far this conception of the advent of an Anointed King was justified by the original words of the writers, on whose authority it claimed to rest. Nor are we concerned with any argument as to the greater credibility of those transcendental views which were gradually developed from, and substituted for, the dream of a great Hebrew monarchy having its capital in Jerusalem. To understand aright the ideas and the aspirations of the contemporaries of

Rabbi Jeshua, we are obliged to endeavour to comprehend their thoughts as to the national future. And while we cannot fail to perceive that the Messiah was to them not far different from the awakened champion whose coming was once expected by so many of the Ayran tribes, we are equally made aware of the fact that no Messiah such as the Jews expected in the days of Rabbi Jeshua has ever as yet appeared to rule his people. Never have the chosen race rejected, nor could they ever reject, such a King as they expected. Created by the pride, the faith, the devotion of the national character, nursed by the woes and bitter miseries of their history, implanted as an ineradicable longing in the breasts of generation after generation, the great hope has endured for twenty centuries among the scattered outcasts of the most wonderful of nations; and while the Jew remains a Jew, even to the end of time, he will still yearn for, and still patiently await the coming of the Messiah.

CHAPTER V.

RABBI JESHUA'S LIFE.

The Lake of Kinnereth—The fisherman—Rabbi Jeshua's kith and kin—The neglected peasantry—Miracles—Remarkable cures—Influence of will—Messianic claims—Sorcery—Rabbi Jeshua's disciples—Distrust and love—Ascetic life of Rabbi Jeshua—His celibacy—Summary.

BETWEEN dark precipitous cliffs which are mirrored in its calm blue waves the little lake of Kinnereth lies shining in the afternoon sun. On the south we look to the broad vale of Jordan; on the east to the white walls of limestone, where Gamala stands perched on its camel-like hummock, and above which stretches the broad plateau of Bethania. On the west, in the shadow of the great precipices, stands the new city which Antipas has named in honour of Tiberius; and beyond it, in the dim distance, the walled town of Beth-Tarak projecting into the lake. Northwards we look towards the black lava-fields of Caphar Ahim, and perceive the turbid river entering the lake near the village newly dubbed with the name Julias. Here along the shelving pebbly beach the dark bushes of the oleander shine with their rosy blossoms, and tiny bays and creeks succeed one another, while the great wall of the Galilean mountains towers high above the valley, and the sacred town of Tziphoth gleams on the mountain side.

Close to the brink of the water the hamlet of Capharnahum, with its mud cabins and its little new-built synagogue, spreads beneath the low cliff, where the Roman guard-house is stationed beside the highway; and westwards from the village the rich broad plain of Kinnereth, watered by the mountain streams, green with vines and fig-trees, and waving with graceful palms, stretches to the olive groves above Migdol, and to the great blue fountain beneath, which tradition reported to run below the earth from the fertile Nile itself to this favoured paradise of the "Prince's Garden."

On the brink of the lake stands a stalwart figure —a brown peasant, stripped to the waist, and carrying on his shoulder a basket of rushes. His gaze is intently fixed on the shining water, where his practised eye sees the shadowy shoal silently gliding towards him. Crouching like a tiger, and stepping daintily into the rippling waves, he advances breast high into the sea, and with one sudden effort casts from his arm the great disk of net, which, whirling forward for a few yards, sinks suddenly with a splash beneath the surface, and catches the unwary fish under the dome-shaped cages of its meshes. Quickly drawn to shore, the white sides and gleaming scales of the great breams and sheat-fish glitter in the sunlight on the sand, and the small are divided from the great, the clean from the unclean, before the fisher wanders further along the shore in search of another shoal.

Such was the scene where Rabbi Jeshua's days were oftenest spent, such were the men of his kith and kin with whom he lived and by whom he was beloved. From the fishes of that sea, from the great cast-nets, from the storms which sweep down the mountain gulleys across the lake, from the fields, the flowers, and the flocks of the mountains between which it lies embosomed, he drew the imagery of his poetry, and the fables which went to the hearts of his simple hearers.

Here from the lips of the village priest he had learned his first lessons in the Law ; here, in the loneliness of unsuspected genius, he pondered over the thoughts which made him at length a master in Israel.

To this mountain lake also he returned from the southern deserts to which, under the influence of

Hanan the hermit, he had for a time retreated. Hanan had met his fate—decoyed to the fortress of Mekor. The great throngs which had been gathered by his eloquence into the Vale of Jordan were no longer collected by the river's brink, and Judea no longer condescended to learn from a prophet of Galilee.

Conscious of the power within him, of genius chastened by ascetic probation, and full of the great message which there was none now left to declare to men since Hanan was no more, Jeshua has Saddik—once the learned Rabbi, but now the zealous convert of the Hasaya—returned to his native land to take upon him the fallen mantle of his master.

Few indeed were the disciples capable of understanding the great mind of him who thus came among them. A degraded race of Asiatic Greeks —idolaters and despisers of the chosen people— were to be found in the newly populated cities of Decapolis and at Tiberias. A few semi-heathen courtiers of Antipas, a rustic rabbi or two, represented the gentry of the region. It was not among such that the words of Rabbi Jeshua were likely to find acceptance.

Along the shores of the sea, in their mud cabins and huts of rushes, the poor fishers and husbandmen of Kinnereth lived uncared for and untaught. Along the slopes of the mountains wandered the herdsmen, almost as brutish as their charges, their language a barbarous dialect, which the sarcastic citizen of Jerusalem found it hard to understand. The pestilence of marshy fever smote them in autumn year by year; the damps of winter cramped their limbs with palsy; the glare of the white rock blinded their eyes with ophthalmia; the sun smote them at noonday, and the moon by night with madness, which they believed to be possession by demons. In the dry places, and among the rocky cells of the tombs, they wandered in their fury, half famished and naked. No man cared for the beasts of the people, and no teacher had been so bold as to hope for an immortality of happiness for their souls. The Pharisees crowded each sabbath in the squalid synagogues of the villages; but on the mountains, and beneath the shady terebinths, the poor bowed down in ignorance to the primeval powers of the stars in heaven.

Was it among such a peasantry that the great scholar, the poet, the devout ascetic, the pure-minded and gentle Rabbi might hope to find a hearing? True, they were of his kith and kin these fishers and humble craftsmen of Galilee, yet in education and in genius how far was he removed from them. How among such disciples was it possible that the nobility of his nature and the truth of his perceptions could find a real appreciation?

Nevertheless, there was between himself and his hearers even of the humblest class a bond which no other teacher possessed. There was a secret spring which he could touch, but which the learned Pharisee and the fanatical ascetic alike had failed, or had not cared to find.

Rabbi Jeshua loved the people. He saw in his deep pity that they strayed as the flocks on the mountains whose shepherd was slain by the Arab robber; they wandered listlessly as the fishes which no net had gathered in; they grew up like the tares in the fields where the enemy alone gathers his harvest, or as the self-sown grain on the housetops, destined to be hereafter cast into the oven of Gehenna; and on the poor of the land Rabbi Jeshua had compassion.

The little hamlet of Capharnahum stretched along the flat shore almost to the water's edge, and rose on the side of the great knoll to the east. The mud cabins surrounded the little rudely-built synagogue of stone, with its whitewashed dome newly repaired at the expense of a Roman centurion commanding the little detachment of Syrian auxiliaries. The beautiful structures which Bar Jochai erected nearly a century later in Galilee were not yet in existence, and the villagers were proud of their synagogue, mean and humble though it was.

In one of those dark and narrow huts Rabbi Jeshua sat resting, with his followers around him. In the shadow of the bare mud-walled room, the white garments and ample turban of the Master, the brown-striped mantles, the sheepskin jackets, the bronzed and naked limbs of his peasant pupils, formed a picture such as Rembrandt would have loved to paint. The circle of listeners crouched on the clay floor or on the rude reed mats, almost filled the narrow space round the holy man. The doorway was choked with the forms of those who sought admission, and in the fierce glare of the sunlight the throngs of poor crowded to gain a glimpse of the great physician.

The blue-robed women brought their sick babies in their arms, the ophthalmic patients groped to the door, the withered limbs and fevered faces of the sick met the eye on all sides; and as the cool evening time commenced, and the red glow spread over lake and mountain, the beds of the sufferers were carried out, and laid in the path by which the Rabbi must pass.

Simeon records an instance of yet more eager anxiety. On one occasion, he says, the mud roof and thatch of boughs which covered in the little cabin were torn up by impatient friends, and the poor nervous sufferer was lowered into the midst of the circle close to the very feet of Rabbi Jeshua. He records, moreover, that so great was the patient's faith in the power of the Master, that he was able to obey the imperative command of the Rabbi, who adjured him to rise and walk.

Again a wonderful story is related in another part of the chronicle. From Capharnahum the Master and his followers rowed over the still lake to the mountains of Hippos near Bethania. As they landed and toiled up the steep rocky path, a fearful figure greeted their sight. The tall lean form, the ragged beard, the long hair unkempt and tangled, the naked body burnt brown by the sun and bruised and cut by the rocks, the fierce and grim countenance, betokened a savage maniac. It was the madman who inhabited the rocky sepulchres above the pass, whom many had vainly striven to bind with chains, and who came running and bounding over the rocks, uttering inarticulate cries of menace and rage. At sight of him the bystanders fled, the Greek shepherds who were feeding their unclean herds on the acorns of the scattered oaks were infected with the panic, and the rush of the crowd frightened even the black swine, who galloped hastily off, and falling over the precipices perished in the lake.

Yet when the followers of Rabbi Jeshua ventured back to the spot, expecting no doubt to find only his mangled remains torn by the devils who possessed the madman, they were awe-stricken to see him seated calmly, and that wild figure at his feet, conquered by the soothing influence of all-mastering will, "clothed, and in his right mind."

In reading the quaint chronicle of Simeon has Saddik, we are no doubt at liberty to receive, with the scepticism which we may consider a sign of our infinite superiority to himself, the various wonderful statements which he makes respecting the actions of Rabbi Jeshua. We are not dealing with those high questions of miracle which form the subject of controversy between the great doctors of the Church and the great critics of the world; and while acknowledging that such miracles, if attested by the evidence of inspiration, are binding on us as articles of faith, we are not thereby forbidden to criticise freely the statements of a rabbinical chronicler any more than we are forbidden to denounce the errors of the modern spiritualist or clairvoyant. We are dealing with a simple episode of Oriental life, with the spirit of Eastern superstition among the illiterate peasantry of Galilee, and among the humble scribes of the Hasaya. It is a question of evidence, and none will suppose that in thus freely criticising the ideas of our quaint author, we are denying great truths of the miraculous surely attested by inspiration, if inspiration ever did attest a miracle.

Yet let us pause before contemptuously dismissing the stories which crowd the pages of Simeon's chronicle. One fact we cannot doubt: Rabbi Jeshua attained suddenly to a fame, of which the noise spread from Dan to Beersheba; and among the small band of his personal adherents he was secretly believed to be the expected Messiah. How are we to account for this sudden reputation? Preachers and prophets, rabbis and hermits, there were enough and to spare. Simeon does not even pretend that the exquisite fables of Rabbi Jeshua were understood by his astonished audience; nor did they contain any very great or revolutionary doctrine, or utter any new cry, other than those which formed the burden of every prophet and every doctor of the Law. That a rabbi should do otherwise than turn with contempt from the peasant and the sinner may have created surprise and awakened personal attachment. That a hermit should mingle with the village crowd, might be explained on the assumption that he was mad, or (which was much the same) inspired—an object of reverence partly, and partly of pity; but these peculiarities are not sufficient to account for the ringing voice of rumour throughout the length and breadth of the land.

Perhaps, then, Rabbi Simeon's explanation is after all the simplest. He tells us that Rabbi Jeshua wrought wonderful cures among the people of the land; that he healed the possessed, gave sight to the blind, made the lame walk, opened the ears of the deaf, cured the leper and the palsied, nay, even raised the dead.

We might easily explain this all away, or we might say that after so long a time, and with so meagre an account, it is now impossible to form a judgment as to what really occurred. We might point out that there were reasons which made it necessary for the followers of this supposed Messiah to pretend that he possessed supernatural powers. In various ways we might apply the cynical scepticism of modern Western scientific criticism to the simple narrative of this humble writer; and those who consider the question unworthy their attention will no doubt here close the present volume.

Nevertheless, suspicion often overreaches itself, and wisdom is not always incredulous of the honesty of the simple. We know that the physician enjoys yet in the East a reputation to which not even the prophet can attain; that his simplest cures are attributed to a supernatural cunning, or to the aid of mighty spirits who obey him. We know that the faith of his patients often secures the success of the treatment. We know yet more that the blessings and heartfelt gratitude of the poor, the sick, the mother and the wife, the old and young, follow him wherever he goes, and circle him round as a wall of defence. Let those who know not the East think of the doctor among the passages of an Irish court in London, and imagine the faith and the affection which are given to the physician in Syria, among a peasantry more ignorant, more neglected, and more credulous than even the lowest caste of the English poor.

Remember also that the knowledge of medicine was among the mysterious attainments of the monastic Hasaya. What simple craft in herbs and unguents Rabbi Jeshua may have possessed we known not; but this we know, that in vain might he have striven to explain to those whom he healed, the causes—perhaps only half understood by himself—of their cure, and in vain might he have protested—as indeed he did protest—that none but natural means were at his disposal. It was equally possible in their eyes that his secret charms should be made of clay, or that a herbal unguent should be the means of healing the eyes of the ophthalmic patient; and the conviction that, by miraculous means, he exorcised the demons to whom all sickness was plainly attributable, was too deeply imprinted in the minds of his patients, through the influence of universal and long existing superstition, for it to be possible that one man, however honest, and however outspoken, should be able to combat the credulity of the populace.

As regards the raising of the dead, it must be noted that in the only case recorded by Simeon has Saddik the chronicler has honestly stated that Rabbi Jeshua never claimed to have done any such deed. His patient, a young girl, was believed by the bystanders to be deceased; but the penetration of the physician showed him apparently that it was merely a case of a faint, a fit, or such like seizure; and when the crowd had been driven out and air given to the sufferer she revived, not to the surprise of Rabbi Jeshua, but to the boundless astonishment of those who had heard without believing his assertion that she was not really dead.

Still we have to account for those cases in which nervous diseases and possession were healed and controlled by Rabbi Jeshua. As regards both these and the other so-called miraculous cures attributed to him, we have to combat the difficulties that Rabbi Simeon's narrative was written down long after the events recorded had occurred, and that those events are represented according as they appeared to the understanding of a man not less ignorant nor less superstitious than were the humble patients themselves. Yet in spite of the element of wonder thus unconsciously introduced into the story by the chronicler, we find more than once traces of the real spirit in which Rabbi Jeshua himself regarded his own wonderful acts. More than once we find that he declared, to the persons whom he healed, that it was their faith which made them whole.

To a physician this declaration is full of suggestiveness. He knows practically how powerful is the influence of a strong will over the less firm determination of inferior minds. We have degraded this unstudied yet undoubted influence by the names of mesmerism or electro-biology, we have allowed it to remain the plaything of charlatans and adventurers; yet it will not be questioned that the soothing influence which a strong character exercises over the maniac or the nervous sufferer, may be witnessed in our own times and in our own country not less than it was in the East nineteen centuries ago.

Such cures as are recorded of Rabbi Jeshua have been performed by men who have laid no claim to peculiar sanctity or to supernatural power, for we are at least justified in assuming that the supposed possession by demons is but an Oriental synonym for madness. How far those cures were perfect or permanent, or how far they may have been temporary and dependent on the presence of the physician we are unable now to judge; but it is not from the chronicle of Rabbi Simeon that we can draw evidence sufficient to prove that Rabbi Jeshua either possessed, or even claimed to be able to exert, any supernatural powers of healing.

That Rabbi Jeshua did possess that strength of will, and controlling influence, which have been suggested as the cause of his power over nervous patients may perhaps be hereafter judged from the account of his death. It is by such strong natures that the passions of other men are roused—great love in some, fierce hatred on the contrary in others; and such love and such hatred were the fortune of the great Rabbi.

In the little synagogue of Capharnahum the

power of Rabbi Jeshua over the insane was first evinced. Among the fishers of Kinnereth the cures of fever, eyesore, skin-diseases, and nervous affections were first performed. The fame of these good deeds spread like lightning over the land. In a country where medical knowledge was confined to the recommendation of such charms as an adder's skin or a locust's egg, and where all disease was attributed to the malign influence of demons, the glad news was spread abroad that a healing prophet had appeared, and rumour magnified the character of his deeds not less in his lifetime than has tradition in later days.

Among those who knew and loved Rabbi Jeshua the healing power which he possessed was evidence of his prophetic claims. From Elijah downwards the power of raising the dead, of cleansing the leper, of curing the sick, had belonged to those who had found favour with and were inspired by God. But yet more the healing of the sick was one of the special attributes of the expected Messiah; and the Rabbi himself pointed out that by him they saw fulfilled the prediction that the future prince should give sight to the blind and heal the wounded.

In the Babylonian Talmud we find a beautiful fable which, though of later date, may serve to illustrate the Jewish expectations as to the healing powers of the Messiah. "When will he come?" said Rabbi Jehoshua ben Levi. "Go, ask him," answered Elijah. "Where does he abide?" "At the gate of Rome." "And whereby is he known?" "He sits among the poor and sick, and they open all their wounds at once. Yet he only opens and binds one, and then another, for he says, perchance I may be called and may not tarry."

But Rabbi Jeshua had enemies as well as friends. The Pharisees of Jerusalem, refusing to recognise a Galilean Messiah, found an easier way of accounting for his healing powers, and openly accused him of sorcery. The divine Name—the mystic Shemhamphorash—was a potent spell, through the use of which the wizard might compel the powers of evil. In later times it was pretended that Rabbi Jeshua had impiously violated the sanctuary itself, had penetrated into the Holy of Holies, and had read the sacred name written on the stone of foundation. It was through the knowledge thus unlawfully obtained that he was able, said his enemies, to work his wonders.

The answer which Rabbi Jeshua gave to this charge is striking for its simple dignity. In order to work wonders by aid of the Name it was necessary that he should pronounce it according to its letters. Yet so to pronounce it, save when the high priest once a year blessed the people, constituted the crime of blasphemy which according to Jewish law was restricted to this one offence—the utterance of the name Jehovah. Rabbi Jeshua did not deign to protest his innocence of this offence; he merely answered his accusers that, without so doing, he could not through sorcery work the wonders which men attributed to him.

It was, we have already seen, as the successor and disciple of Hanan of Bethania that Rabbi Jeshua commenced his public career. When the voice of the hermit was silenced that of his greater pupil began to be heard. The message which he announced was the same, and not only Rabbi Jeshua but his disciples also took up the cry of the immediate advent of Messiah, and the exhortation to penitence and good works.

But in addition to such preaching Rabbi Jeshua and (to a certain extent) his immediate followers performed we may believe remarkable cures; and gradually the conviction of the Messiahship of the Master changed materially the character of his own mission and influenced the expectations of his adherents. With this subject we shall however be concerned later, when speaking of the maxims of the Rabbi, and may now confine ourselves to the consideration of his early career, of the views of his fellow-countrymen regarding him, and of the peculiarly ascetic character of his life in Galilee.

The disciples of Rabbi Jeshua were derived without exception from the peasant class. One at least seems to have belonged to the ancient and aboriginal population of the Canaanites, and one to the fierce and uncompromising party of the Zealots whose intemperance was destined to bring ruin on the chosen people.

These men, sent out to exhort the populace, and to prepare for the great expected catastrophe, were regarded with supreme contempt by the school of the Pharisees, as rustics to whom even the washing of hands before meals (a mark alike of good breeding and of religious purity) was unknown. But perhaps among the poor of the land to whom their Master had devoted his life, fitter messengers could not be found than were the rough fishers and herdsmen whom Rabbi Jeshua had attached to his person.

By the Pharisees also the newly announced prophet was importuned for a sign or test of his powers. It was a recognised rule in Jewish law that no prophet could be accepted as truly inspired until some prediction of good made by him had been fulfilled; but to such questions Rabbi

Jeshua gave no answer. He knew well how hopeless it must be to endeavour to persuade his enemies, or to seek an honest appreciation of the nobility of his life among the prejudiced fanatics of the Jerusalem colleges. The wondrous cures which he had wrought had been attributed to sorcery, and even if he had consented, or if he had been able, to satisfy his critics by predictions soon after verified, the power of prophecy might in the same manner have been attributed to a demoniacal origin.

Among the members of his own family the claims of the great Rabbi were not recognised. Perhaps no Jew could have been found at any period of history, however eagerly he may have expected the advent of a Messiah, who would have been capable of believing his own brother to be the expected prince. The brethren of Rabbi Jeshua pronounced him mad, and after ineffectual efforts to restrain his actions, they (with exception of the martyr Jacob who became a convert at a later period) left him without pity to the sad fate which, as we shall hereafter see, awaited him.

Among the great orthodox sects whose leaders were to be found in Jerusalem, the sudden reputation of Rabbi Jeshua awakened serious alarm. The Herodians regarded him as a possible revolutionist not less dangerous than Hanan, and the superstitious Antipas even doubted whether it might not be the murdered hermit himself who had been reincarnate, with powers yet more wonderful than before. The Sadducees saw in the teaching of Rabbi Jeshua a menace to the established power of the then dominant family of high priests. The Pharisees only recognised in him a teacher who had pronounced himself independent of the trammels of tradition.

Thus among the powerful, the rich, and the ruling classes the sudden celebrity of the new Master roused only feelings of hatred, fear, and opposition; while among the poor, the despised, the ignorant, and the oppressed the calm wisdom and the deep compassion of this great teacher, who had vouchsafed to humble himself to their estate, awakened sentiments of heartfelt gratitude and ardent love.

The character of Rabbi Jeshua's religious tenets has been variously misrepresented not only by modern writers but even by those who professed to be his followers. He has been represented as a Greek philosopher elaborating a new republican moral system. He has been pictured as a poet delighting in the rural life of Galilee until finally spoiled by adulation and lured by vanity to his fate. German metaphysicians have converted him into a mythical embodyment of abstract virtues. The Pharisees have represented him as a Pharisee, and even the mystic Alexandrians have claimed him as a teacher of Cabbalistic gnosticism.

There are, however, certain broad indications observable in his life and teaching, which show that he continued to adhere to the ascetic habits and to the views of the sect of the Hasaya. His wandering life spent in journeying from village to village, on errands of mercy and for the exhortation of the peasantry; his frequent retreat to the solitary mountains or deserts of Galilee; his knowledge of medicine; his reputation as a prophet; his poverty, and his frequent eulogies of an ascetic life, are among the many incidental indications of his views and habits.

The peasantry of Galilee were a turbulent and fanatical race, yet we never find that Rabbi Jeshua availed himself of the influence which he possessed to stir them up to rebellion against the constituted powers of the realm; for the Hasaya were a sect remarkable for their peaceful submission to the political powers, and in this respect therefore Rabbi Jeshua followed the precepts of the party to which he belonged.

The country round Phahil, south of Kinnereth, and east of the lake, the region of Bethania and the vale of Jordan, formed a district which appears to have been the favourite abode of the Abionim, or "poor," who were akin to the Hasaya. It is to this region that we find Rabbi Jeshua often resorting, and another indication is thus afforded of his real religious tenets.

The Hasaya having certain ceremonies and lustrations peculiar to themselves, were guilty of the neglect of the great feasts of Jerusalem and of the sacrifices commanded by the law. Thus when we find no mention of any visit to the Holy City by Rabbi Jeshua before his final and fatal journey, and when we note that, according to the chronicle of Simeon, the Rabbi then looked for the first time on the great edifices of the capital, we have again an indication that he belonged to the Hasaya.

The independence of doctrine which marks the sayings of the Rabbi sufficiently shows that he belonged neither to the Pharisees nor to the Sadducees, as will be more fully explained later; but one indication of his peculiar asceticism remains to be pointed out.

It was considered by the devout Jew an absolute duty to marry, and to marry early. The Mishna fixes the age of eighteen as the latest at which a man should wed. The first chapter of the Torah contained the command to increase and multiply, and the Jewish mother might always hope to be the happy parent of the Messiah. How then do we account for the fact that Rabbi Jeshua was unmarried, except on the ground that he belonged to the celibate sect of the Hasaya?

The Jewish contempt for women and cynical estimate of their moral worth finds expression in many passages of their ancient literature. The Hasaya were specially remarkable for their distrust of the sex; and while not absolutely condemning all wedlock as wicked, extolled the virtue of celibacy to the highest degree. The views of a future Paradise, which Rabbi Jeshua on one occasion divulged, differed from those of other doctors especially in this, that he spoke neither of marrying nor giving in marriage, and deprived the expected Eden of the materialistic element which has formed so conspicuous a feature of the Moslem Jenneh not less than of the Pharisaic Paradise.

It is true that the Jews never spoke of the Messiah as having a queen, although in a psalm considered to be of Messianic importance such a consort is mentioned. A high priest would, it was thought, stand by the throne of the "Anointed Prince," but a princess was not depicted as sharing that throne. In this respect Rabbi Jeshua's celibacy might be thought to be the result of his

Messianic pretensions rather than of his ascetic views; but such an explanation would not suffice to account for the fact that at thirty years of age, when only just commencing his career, and when probably not as yet claiming to be the Messiah, he was still unwedded; and the former explanation, that he belonged to an ascetic and celibate sect, seems therefore to be more satisfactory.

Here, then, before proceeding to enumerate the recorded sayings of Rabbi Jeshua, and before relating his death or pointing the moral of his career, we may pause to sum up the chief features of his life in Galilee.

He appeared among men as the successor of the hermit Hanan. He took up the burden of the exhortation to penitence and good works, and the prediction of the approaching advent of the Anointed Prince of Israel. He attained among the simple peasantry of the land to a reputation for wisdom, sanctity, and supernatural power, which was due to the purity of his life and the medical knowledge distinctive of his sect. He gained their affections by the tender compassion which he evinced for their sufferings, and by the good deeds which he wrought among them. He earned the hatred and distrust of the higher orders by the superiority to class prejudices which he manifested in his treatment of the poor, and by the novelty of some of his doctrines on traditional and religious questions. He was cast off by his family, accused of sorcery by the Pharisees, and importuned to give proof of the prophetic character which had been thrust upon him rather than assumed by him. The elements of a great future struggle with constituted authority were perceptible; yet in the tenor of his daily life there was no trace of that spirit of rebellion against the ruling powers which was so marked a characteristic of the Galilean fanatics of his time.

We may picture to ourselves the little band of ascetics who travelled barefoot, and clad each in a single garment, across the rugged ridges of Upper Galilee or through the dark brown plains of Sepphoris. We may recall to the mind's eye the eager crowds of tanned peasants, the blue-robed women, the naked children, who pressed round the Master, intent not so much on listening to his exhortations or to his mysterious fables, as on bringing to his notice the sick child, the withered limb, the sightless eyes of a relative or friend. On the shore they crowded round the little boat in which he sat apart. In the village they tore up even the brushwood roof of the cabin where he sat, to lower the palsied into the midst of the attendant circle of his listeners.

Conspicuous by his spotless turban, his white garment, his distinctive girdle, by the beauty of his features, by the calm dignity of his manner, the great Master moved among them all. Patiently he listened to their troubles, healed their ills, and instructed their ignorance; but among these humble followers, who heard with their ears but understood not the beautiful fables which he uttered, there was no man who could comprehend the genius, or fathom the wisdom of the teacher. Alone in his greatness, and removed as far from the rabbinic doctor as from the untaught peasant, Rabbi Jeshua moved among his fellow-countrymen in the solitude of genius, distinguished from all other teachers in his self-created vocation—the Messiah of the Poor.

CHAPTER VI.

SAYINGS OF RABBI JESHUA.

Rabbinical maxims—Rabbi Jeshua's peculiar views—The praise of poverty—Fanaticism—The Sabbath—Fasting—Divorce — Tribute—Washing — Immortality — Fables—Messianic claims—Concealment—Genealogy— Fatalism—Oriental character.

WHEN the heathen scoffer came to Shammai and asked to be taught the Law in such time as he could remain standing on one leg, the vice-president of the Sanhedrim dismissed him in great anger. But when he made the same demand of Hillel, the answer was:

"Do not to others what you would not that others should do to you. This is the whole Law, the rest is only a comment on this."

"Thou shalt love thy neighbour as thyself." In these words likewise Hillel was wont to epitomise the Law. Yet, curiously enough, both these sayings have been attributed to Rabbi Jeshua, and supposed to be original, although the latter, at least, is merely a paraphrase of a passage in the Pentateuch itself.

Many other sayings are common to Rabbi Jeshua, and to other doctors who were his contemporaries or his predecessors.

"Do His will as if it were thine own will, that He may fulfil thy will as His own will," was a saying of Gamaliel.

"Judge not," was the advice of Hillel; and to him also are attributed the maxims, "He that exalteth himself shall be abased," "If I do no good works, who shall do them for me?"

The repetition of such sayings is not, however, sufficient to prove that Rabbi Jeshua was a disciple of Hillel, or of the Jerusalem rabbinical school. The maxims do not contain any statement of startling originality or of metaphysical importance. They are rather reflections arising from a careful study of the Law, and from a right appreciation of its spirit and intention, and are thus likely to have been independently uttered by students who were mutually unknown one to the other.

The maxims of Rabbi Jeshua must indeed be considered as altogether secondary in importance to the facts of his career, and as such they are regarded by the chronicler, who, while jotting down here and there in his brief record of events such sayings or parables as had most firmly fixed themselves in his memory, admits that many others which he has not preserved were spoken by the Rabbi.

If, then, it may be asked, the sayings of this rabbi are so little different from those of his contemporaries, of what interest is his career beyond that of other Jewish doctors who, however well known to the curious student of Talmudic literature, are but obscure names in the history of their age, and have left no impress of their influence on the world in general?

The answer must be that the interest of the life of Rabbi Jeshua lies in his actions rather than his words; and, moreover, that in two important points his teaching is entirely distinct from that of his contemporaries: namely, first, his doctrine as to the poor and ignorant; and, secondly, his doctrine as to the expected Messiah, whom he claimed to be.

The teaching of Rabbi Nitai, of Arbela, commanded the student to "withdraw from an evil neighbour and not to associate with the wicked." Yet Rabbi Jeshua, who lived two centuries later than this great authority, was in daily contact with sinners, and never shunned the society of his neighbour, however fallen away from ceremonial righteousness.

"A boor cannot fear sin, nor can a peasant become a saint," was the opinion of Hillel. Yet Rabbi Jeshua consorted with the peasantry far more than with the devout, and announced himself more than once to be the prophet of the lost sheep of the flock of Israel.

"Get thyself a master," said Joshua Ben Perakiah, the contemporary of Alexander Jannæus, and the same maxim is recorded of Gamaliel. Yet the Galilean Rabbi was ambitious to become a master rather than to find one, and is said to have spoken in a tone of authority and originality very different from that of the students who (like a modern Moslem preacher) traced back every covenant or interpretation which they repeated, from one authority to another up to the inspired original exposition of Ezra himself. Rabbi Jeshua gave to his hearers not the tradition of a certain school, but his own deductions from a deep and intelligent study of the Law of Moses; and while on the one hand it is wrong to suppose that his maxims on questions of morality were entirely original— founded as they were on the authority of the Scriptures—it seems, on the other hand, equally erroneous to suppose that he belonged to either of the great Pharisaic schools which were then contending in Jerusalem.

Like other doctors, then, Rabbi Jeshua advocated peace, humility, charity, good works, submission to lawful authority, forgiveness of injuries, and the abnegation of self-will. Like other rabbis, he couched his teaching in fables; and like them also he addressed his Hebrew hearers as children of God.

On the other hand, his treatment of the Law is marked by an originality which distinguishes his utterances from those of any school of the day, although there is apparently nothing in his doctrine which could be considered as plainly irreconcilable with the words of Moses.

This view of the doctrines of Rabbi Jeshua is supported by many instances in which maxims supposed by most writers to be his original ideas, may be compared with the passages in the Law from which they were derived. The radical difference between Rabbi Jeshua's views and those of other doctors as regarded the teaching of the peasantry, was moreover but a feature of the mild philosophy of the Hasaya, who, while approaching the Pharisees in their regard for tradition, were distinguished, as Josephus and Philo relate, by their love of peace, poverty, and seclusion, their contempt for riches and for the ambitions of the world.

In the maxims of Rabbi Jeshua we find indeed expressed some of the best-known tenets of the Hasaya and of the Abionim. The praise of celibacy and chastity was one of their distinguishing and least orthodox doctrines. They were instructed to wear their garments to rags, and their shoes into holes before buying new ones, to bathe frequently in cold water, to have all things in common, to travel from city to city, to heal the sick, to exhort the worldly.

It is, then, in the light of an acquaintance with the views of these humble pietists that we must regard many of the doctrines of Rabbi Jeshua, for to his wandering emissaries he enjoined chastity and celibacy, the rites of ablution, the contempt for wealth. He bade them wear only the single garment which distinguished the poor peasant from the rich citizen clad in his closely-fitting upper gaberdine. He enjoined on them to go barefoot, as the poorest of the poor, or shod with the sandals of desert wanderers. "Blessed are the needy, the sad, the lowly, the hungry, the merciful, the pure, the peaceful, the persecuted, for to them are given the times of the Messiah." Such were his words, and such were the doctrines of the Hasaya hermits, who had preceded and who followed him. It was the ideal of that unknown prophet of the captivity, whose description of himself—applied later by the Jews to the Messiah—represented the shepherd of wandering sheep, the man of sorrows, despised and rejected, afflicted and poor, preaching to the meek, and comforting the broken in heart.

The advice which was offered to the rich by the great puritan of Galilee was couched in a similar strain. They were to sell their goods and give away their patrimony to the poor. It was, perhaps, rather in view of the speedy coming of the Messiah, the necessity of doing some good work before that day should arrive, the transient nature of all worldly advantages in consequence of the impending change, than because of any radical or communistic ideas on his own part, that such advice was given; but the ring of the Hasaya asceticism echoes through the exhortation — the desire for treasure in heaven, the contempt for riches on earth.

Rabbi Simeon records an instance in which a young Pharisee, one of the sect of the "inquirers," as they were called, who made it a custom to ask others to point out to them their faults, demanded of the Rabbi in what respect he had failed in devout obedience to the law. The answer was, that until he had sold all for the poor he had not fulfilled the injunctions of the command, "thou shalt not harden thy heart nor shut thy hand against thy poor brother." Such advice was no doubt unpalatable to the rich Pharisee, whose religion was but a refined selfishness; but Rabbi Jeshua condemned, without scruple, all who hesitated to go to the same lengths with himself in the zealous pursuit of holiness.

Traces of that stern fanaticism, which appears to be inseparable from the religious enthusiasm of the East, are indeed not wanting in the sayings of the Galilean Rabbi. Not only the rich were condemned, but those who spared father or mother, sister or brother, who shrank from the most appalling sacrifice of natural affection, or from the loss of life or limb in the cause of the faith, were alike pronounced unworthy of a place in the future kingdom of God. It is true that the sacrifices which he demanded were perhaps more difficult for the rich and prosperous than for the poor and needy; yet in spite of the tender pity which Rabbi Jeshua evinced for the sinners whom he addressed, we find often that the standard of conduct which he placed before his followers, as an ideal, was one which has been recognised by the world in all ages as impracticably exalted, and beyond the capacity of human frailty to attain.

On many questions of the day or of sectarian

difference, Rabbi Jeshua had a strong opinion of his own. To us these questions are for the most part of little interest. But, like other great men, he was but little in advance of the spirit of his time. The relative proportions of things appeared to his mind according to the importance which early education and immediate surroundings had originally given to them. A leader, whose mind is so remotely divided from that of his followers as to dull and weaken his interest in those things which are to them of primary importance, cannot hope to influence in a marked manner the thought and actions of his fellows, however much his superiority may be recognised later, by men of more advanced intellect and education.

Rabbi Jeshua was a man of his own times. Educated in the tenets of Jewish faith, he looked forward, as did others, to a Messiah whose advent might be immediately expected. Brought up in the belief that only in the Law of Moses was the whole and finite sum of truth to be found, he devoted his energies to the right understanding of that Law rather than to any independent and original search after truth. Accustomed from his childhood to connect the acquisition of wealth with oppression, injustice, corruption, and deceit, he was naturally inclined to believe that only through poverty and asceticism could the temptations of the world be avoided, and the indispensable holiness of a perfect life be attained.

Thus to Rabbi Jeshua the questions which then agitated the Jewish world, assumed an importance with which we find it hard to sympathise; yet, as illustrating the views with which he regarded life in general, they have still some interest for the reflective mind. The observance of the sabbath, fasting, divorce, the payment of tribute, the washing of hands, such were the subjects concerning which fierce disputes were raging among the doctors in the time of Rabbi Jeshua. To the philosophic Roman of the day, no less than to the philosophic Englishmen of our own times, such matters of the Jew's superstition may have appeared too puerile to be seriously discussed by men of mature intellect; but to the Oriental, whose religion is the very essence of his daily life, such questions were, and are, of greater importance than any matters of merely worldly interest could possibly claim to be.

There was, perhaps, no instance in which the self-torturing ingenuity of anxious obedience had more completely frustrated the original intentions of the Law of Moses than in the observance of the sabbath. Designed as a day of rest, of worship, and of recreation, it became, under the direction of the Pharisees, a continually recurring period of discomfort and inconvenience. The very slightest semblance of work was prohibited; but the law which forbade a Jew to travel more than two thousand cubits was evaded by a complicated system of legal fictions, which only find a parallel in the modern Arab evasions of the law of the Koran. It is true that the instinct of self-preservation had induced the Hasmoneans to justify self-defence against the heathen on the sabbath; but short of the danger of life, no necessity was allowed to supersede the law of the sabbath. Perhaps the day of rest may have been somewhat less dismal than the dreary Sundays of our Northern fellow-countrymen, inasmuch as the wearing of ornaments, and indulgence in harmless recreation, or exercise in the open air, were not forbidden. But, on the other hand, the Jews were far more thorough than the most devout Scot can claim to be, in their abstention even from any act which might be classed as a "son of works." Mechanical action might not be set in motion so as to continue through the sabbath. A tailor might not carry his needle on his person, nor might the net of the fowler remain spread after the sabbath eve. At Tiberias, a pipe of cold spring water was carried through the hot baths, and thus gave a warm supply; yet the liquid thus heated by the action of a natural agent was unlawful for drinking or washing on the sabbath. "The cow of Rabbi Eleazar was led forth with a strap between her horns (which, it was argued, might have been tied to them on the sabbath), but it was contrary to the will of the wise men."

"Whoever brings out food, even the size of a dried fig, is guilty of death." Such was the stern decision of the doctors, and such dicta were no doubt enforced on all over whom the Sanhedrim had authority.

Boldly to break through the trammels of such a bondage, to set at nought the devices which had gained authority through long custom, was no doubt to the Jew, as to the Moslem of our own days, a moral impossibility. Subterfuges, legal fictions, equivocations, and dexterous perversions of the plain words of the Law, were recognised as allowable; but there was, no doubt, a certain originality in the view which—reverting to the true spirit of the institution—Rabbi Jeshua enunciated, in the pithy maxim that "the sabbath was made for man, and not man for the sabbath."

The question of fasting was, in like manner, one which distinguished the followers of Rabbi Jeshua from the Pharisees. By fasting, we must understand, not the voluntary abstinence of individual ascetics, but the national fasts proclaimed by the Sanhedrim, in addition to those annually observed in obedience to the Law. Fasting, moreover, as explained in the Talmud, appears to have been similar among the Jews to the modern fasting of Orientals in Ramadan. Thus, while neither food nor drink might pass the lips during the day time of a fast, flesh and wine might be eaten and drunk after nightfall, excepting on the occasion of the great day of Atonement, when even children were to be induced, if possible, to fast.

The annual fasts, and those specially proclaimed in times of drought, pestilence, or public calamity, do not appear to have been observed by the Hasaya, although the frugality of their ordinary habits might well be contrasted with the intemperance of other sects during the great feasts. Rabbi Jeshua claimed such independence for his disciples, on the ground that the new expected order dispensed with the traditional observances authorised by the Sanhedrim. His maxim was couched in language which resembles that used at a later period by the famous Rabbi Meier. "Look not at the flask, but at that which is therein," said Rabbi Meier, "for there are new flasks full of old wine; and old flasks which have not even new wine in them." A somewhat similar figure of Rabbi Jeshua's is recorded, to the effect that the strong wine of a freshly fermenting enthusiasm might not be safely trusted in the old flask of an effete formalism, lest it should burst out and be spilled.

The abuse of the power of divorce—which remained as little restricted as in the primitive age of Moses, was also undoubtedly a crying evil of the day. Those who are familiar with the domestic life of the modern Jews of the East, will know how prejudicial an influence to the happiness of women is the constant terror of capricious divorce, with its consequent separation from child and home. The condemnation of such conduct which Rabbi Jeshua pronounced was sweeping and unqualified. He agreed, it is true, with the school of Shammai, against that of Hillel, in allowing only one reason as justifying divorce, but his argument was founded on the words of the earliest dictum of the Law: "Therefore shall a man leave his father and his mother and cleave unto his wife."

No less delicate was the question of paying tribute to foreign and heathen rulers, among a race whose sacred literature belonged mainly to a time when they had enjoyed independence. The Herodian party with whom the Pharisees were in league, and the Sadducees who had accepted the rule of the Romans, were alike interested in a settlement of this question which might reconcile their consciences with their practice; but the fierce Zealots of Galilee, who refused to recognise any king, Hebrew or heathen, native or foreign, save only Jehovah Himself, were the compatriots of Rabbi Jeshua, who might reasonably be suspected to share their sentiments. The Hasaya, however, were a peaceful people, who sought to solve questions in which religious principles clashed with political expedience, by retreat to the seclusion of the desert, rather than by violent revolutionary attempts; and in consequence of this spirit Rabbi Jeshua safely escaped the snares of his crafty enemies, when they endeavoured to entangle him into a declaration of rebellion against the existing rule of the Cæsar.

Yet more offensive in the eyes of the Pharisees was the neglect of ceremonial purifications on the part of the followers of Rabbi Jeshua. Tradition prescribed that half a wineglassful of water (and no more) should be poured on the hands before meals. It mattered not that frequent and copious ablutions were used by the followers of the Hasaya, for in the eyes of the Pharisees those who neglected this simply ceremonial purification were as unclean as though they had touched a house smitten with leprosy, or had held in their hands a sacred copy of the Law; for by some extraordinary process of reasoning the contact of a scroll written in the sacred characters was considered to necessitate a similarly infinitesimal cleansing of the hands.

In most of these questions Rabbi Jeshua was directly opposed to the great traditional schools of the Pharisees; yet could he not, on the other hand, be classed among their adversaries the Sadducees; for while he denounced, with vehemence and contempt, the hollow formalism and hypocrisy of those who, in following the letter, had forgotten the spirit of the Law, he equally condemned the materialism of their Saducean opponents and held firmly the belief which characterized the Hasaya that "the immortal souls of men imprisoned in their bodies should when released from their bondage mount upwards with joy." Yet in combating the grotesque ideas of the followers of Sadok and Boethus, Rabbi Jeshua could find no text in the Pentateuch on which to base his belief, and his argument is worthy rather of the subtle casuistry of the Pharisees than of the noble simplicity of his other expositions of Scripture. The maxim of Antigonus of Sochoh was indeed, in this matter, more admirable than anything which was said later respecting that doctrine of future punishment and reward which had been gradually introduced into the Jewish moral system.

"Be not," said the successor of Simon the Just, "as servants who serve their master for reward, but be as servants who serve without regard to recompense."

The views which have thus been briefly noticed as expressed in the maxims of Rabbi Jeshua were enunciated from time to time as occasions presented themselves or questions were asked. Profound as was his knowledge of the Law, his utterances were fragmentary, and without connection, and no great ethical system, no strikingly novel views of morality, nothing, in short, beyond the teaching of the Law of Moses as studied according to its original spirit, is found in the sayings of Rabbi Jeshua.

Noble and clear as were his words, it was not on his teaching that his fame rested in his lifetime, and it was the triumph of Messiah, not the development of a new religious system, which formed the true ambition of his career.

Some attempt has been made in the Jerusalem chronicle to present an epitome of the teaching of Rabbi Jeshua in the form of a pretended exhortation delivered on the mountains near Tiberias;

but no such sermon occurs in the artless narrative of Simeon, and in the chronicle of Rabbi Saul it is cut into sections, and distributed over various occasions. The teaching is, moreover, coloured in each account by the peculiar views of the writers; and while there is nothing that is irreconcilable with the tenets of the Hasaya, there is in the Jerusalem chronicle a tone of Pharisaic narrowness, and in the work of Rabbi Saul a leaven of heathen latitudinarianism which suggest a late origin for many maxims attributed to Rabbi Jeshua.

In the same manner a prayer is mentioned by these writers which the Master, like other rabbis, is said to have taught to his pupils. It contains a petition for the coming of Messiah, and expresses the simple desires of the meek Hasaya. Possibly it is a genuine record of the Rabbi's devotions; but Simeon does not notice it as having been composed by his master, and the common superstitious belief in an evil power seeking to injure the pious, occurs at the close of the prayer. Not improbably, therefore, the production of a later disciple has been here attributed to Rabbi Jeshua.

The time-honoured and wise device of presenting a familiar and homely parallel to those whose powers of thought are limited by the narrow perspective of a deficient education, has commended itself to all who have sought to sway the lowest class, and who have understood the existence of that fund of mother wit which characterises the intelligence of the simple and illiterate.

From the common sights of a country life, from the ordinary actions of the fishers of the lake and the tillers of the fields, Rabbi Jeshua drew the imagery of his fables ; and to the springing of the harvest, or the luxuriant growth of the wild herbs of the wilderness, he likened the silent preparation with which, through exhortation and doctrine, he aimed at making all men ready for the great advent of the Messiah.

In the use of such fables on the part of Rabbi Jeshua, there was, however, nothing specially original or remarkable From the days when Jotham, on the summit of Gerizim, contemptuously likened his murderous brother Abimelech to the bramble who was king in Lebanon ; from the time when Joash, king of Israel, replied to his rival of Judah with the celebrated sarcasm, "there came by a wild beast that was in Lebanon, and trode down the thistle," the use of parables had been familiar to the Jewish mind. The answer which Hillel gave to those who questioned the authority of tradition was not unworthy of Socrates himself,

"How knowest thou," he said, "that this is an *Aleph*, and this a *Beth?*" "Because," said his assailant, "we have so learned from our teachers and forefathers." . "If thou acceptedst this in faith," said Hillel, "so also accept the traditions of the Law."

The old story of the clever fox and his dull-witted dupe the bear is to be found among the sayings of the famous fabulist, Rabbi Meier; the very tales which we tell to our children in England are in some cases borrowed—like many of our superstitions—from the Jews. The son of Sirach attributes subtle and dark parables to the wise; and a saying of Rabbi Tarphon, closely resembling one of the recorded similes of Rabbi Jeshua, has been preserved in these words: "The day is short, the labour is mighty; the labourers are slothful; yet the reward is great, and the master of the house presseth for despatch." Or, in the words of Rabbi Jeshua's simile, "The harvest truly is plenteous, but the labourers are few."

While thus indicating the points of similarity or of contrast between the views of Rabbi Jeshua and those of his contemporaries; and while pointing out that his teaching was not so much original as purely representative of the true spirit of the Law of Moses, we have for the moment left out of consideration the claim which the Rabbi advanced to the character of the expected Messiah. But this pretension undoubtedly formed the cardinal difference between himself and every other rabbi of his times.

More than one Messiah had appeared at this epoch of Jewish history. Judas of Golan, the fierce Zealot, whose unconquerable love of freedom brought destruction on his followers; Theudas, the false prophet, who undertook, like Elisha, to strike the waters of Jordan, that his adherents might pass over dryshod, were both the contemporaries of Rabbi Jeshua. Like him, they fell victims to their zeal for a revival of national independence: yet unlike him, on the other hand, they expected by their own power, rather than by aid of divine interposition, to attain the great aims of their lives.

As regards the claims of Rabbi Jeshua to be recognised as the expected Messiah, we have to take into consideration the embarrassing circumstance that the chronicle which we possess was written long after the death of the Rabbi. It is extremely difficult accurately to estimate the effect — conscious or unconscious—on the writer, of the actual development of events. It is possible that the predictions attributed to the Rabbi may have been materially enlarged or modified, in accordance with the subsequent facts: that with the ordinary licence of Oriental literature, so-called prophecies, never actually uttered, may have been inserted into the narrative, and that minute details may have obtained an unnatural importance through the supposed connection which they may have had with the fulfilment of Scriptural prophecies.

On the other hand, it is clear that Rabbi Jeshua could not have done otherwise than expect opposition and hatred from the Pharisees, who had already accused him of sorcery; or from the Sadducees, whose chiefs held the reins of that power which he aimed at destroying. The foresight of his genius must inevitably have suggested that nothing but trouble, suffering, and defeat was likely to attend his efforts, unless assisted by some supernatural interference.

By such forebodings Rabbi Jeshua's conceptions of the character and career of the Messiah seem to have been influenced, and by such facts the statements of his chronicler seem to be unmistakably affected. Many passages of Scripture to which the Jews usually attached no meaning connected with the Messiah were considered by Rabbi Jeshua and his followers to foreshadow a period of suffering and humiliation to be undergone by the Anointed One before the day of his final triumph.

"He came unto his own, and they received him not." "He was despised and rejected of men." "He was numbered with the transgressors." Such were the sayings which his disciples brought forward, as explaining the ill-success of their Master, and the incredulity of the nation respecting his mission. It was a common belief that Messiah should be concealed for a time on earth, and recognised only in the day of his final triumph over the world; and after his death his sorrowful followers adduced, in evidence of the certain fulfilment of their fond expectation of his return, that wonderful passage which tradition ascribed to the pen of Isaiah, in which the servant of the Lord is represented as sacrificed for the sins of others, and as finally obtaining a portion with the great.

It has, however, been already pointed out that such a conception of the career of the Messiah was entirely contrary to the general expectation of the nation; and in many other particulars the views of Rabbi Jeshua as to the Anointed One were equally peculiar. The expectation that Elias must precede Messiah was easily reconciled with the previous career of the prophet Hanan; but the doctrine that the future King was to be the son of David was not so easily explained as referring to Rabbi Jeshua.

At a later period fictitious genealogies were constructed, which traced a descent from David down to Joseph the father of Rabbi Jeshua; but these genealogies, which are entirely discordant among themselves, were never recognised by the true followers of the great Rabbi—the Hasaya and the Abionim. It is probable that the house of David had become extinct centuries before the time of which we treat, and it is certain that Rabbi Jeshua himself never claimed a royal descent. His only recorded utterance on this subject was clearly directed against such a theory. "How say the Scribes that Messiah shall be the son of David? for David calls him Lord, how then can he be his son?" Such was the rabbinic logic whereby he attained to a conclusion entirely at variance with the deductions of the Pharisees from the later prophecies of the sacred books. And in the prophetic passage before mentioned, to which Rabbi Jeshua and his followers were the first to attach a Messianic interpretation, occurs the appropriate exclamation, "Who shall declare his generation?"

The title by which Rabbi Jeshua most commonly called himself was one which was generally supposed to have a Messianic meaning when occurring in the Psalms, or in the book of Daniel—a work which (whenever it may have been composed) had certainly attained to great authority by the time of which we now treat. This title " Son of Man" occurs moreover frequently in that prophecy to which Rabbi Jeshua attached special importance, and the only mark of his habitual assumption of the Messianic dignity lies in the frequent recurrence of this self-description.

As regarded the future of the heathen in the expected kingdom the views of Rabbi Jeshua were broad and charitable, yet founded on authority. To the Messiah the Gentiles were to seek according to Isaiah, and many were the passages of Scripture which might be quoted, as showing that they had their share—though in a subordinate position—in the triumph of the future.

It must be borne in mind that Rabbi Jeshua and his followers were in expectation of an immediately impending change in the condition of the chosen race. It was to no dim future that they looked forward: the kingdom was on the eve of its creation, the Messiah was at the door. They charged men indeed to keep secret the benefits which they had received from the physician, for he was yet in concealment, and the hour had not struck; but it can scarcely be doubted that day by day, week by week, they anxiously scanned the signs of the times, waiting and watching in hope that the hour must come when by divine interposition the claims of their Master would be established.

For it must not be forgotten that, like all Orientals, Rabbi Jeshua was what is called in the West a fatalist. He was not, as some would have us to believe, a philosopher profoundly pondering a moral and ethical system. He was not, as others tell us, a revolutionist or a socialist stirring up class against class, and marshalling the mob against the powers of the realm. Not a politician scheming for a national revival and the expulsion of the foreigner. Not a mystic plunged in deep speculations on the transcendental significance of holy writ. An enthusiast we may perhaps call him, in the sense in which every Oriental is one, namely inasmuch as he had some strong beliefs, was really actuated by religious convictions, and had that capacity for faith which seems so rarely to develop in the Western mind; but in the sense in which enthusiasm is understood among ourselves, as a term of reproach rather than otherwise, as denoting one whose judgment in the common events of life is vitiated by a strong ruling motive or belief, in such a sense Rabbi Jeshua was not even an enthusiast.

Firmly believing in his claim to be considered the future Messiah, he yet never attempted to assert his right to kingly dignity. Profoundly conscious of the dangers which would surround him at the capital, he yet went forward without hesitation to meet his fate. Rejected and despised, he yet remained full of confidence and faith. How can we account for such apparent contradictions, save on the supposition that Rabbi Jeshua fully expected a supernatural manifestation in his favour to be on the eve of occurrence? The hour would strike, the day would dawn, and the long trial of faith and patience would come to a triumphal conclusion. Full of such hope Rabbi Jeshua and his faithful few awaited the future, and in the confidence of a fatalistic belief he went forth to his doom.

The same fundamental difficulty in truly appreciating the motives and expectations of the followers of Rabbi Jeshua confronts us in every incident of his career. It is a difficulty perhaps more conspicuously evident in the writings of those profound German scholars who claim to be the best expositors of the subject than in the works of more modest critics. A difficulty which the modern politician experiences not less than the student of antiquity, namely the incomprehensibility of Oriental thought to the mind of the educated European.

Deep and broad indeed is the line which divides the free intellect of the West from the reverent spirit of the East. It is the contrast of the silence of Oriental noon with the fresh breath of the eddying breezes of the sombre North. Nursed on the tossing billows of our stormy oceans, battling day by day with the forces of nature, the wild Norseman learned that hardy independence of spirit which made him the equal of his jovial gods; but in the quietude of a sultry clime the Hebrew learned only that passive submission to destiny which is the keynote of a fatalistic creed. The "derring do" of the Northman, the "Kismet" of the Arab, are equally characteristic of the tone of their respective natures.

Thus when we compare the East with the West we find submission taking the place of self-reliance, veneration of self-esteem. For freedom we find obedience, for inquiry tradition, for love fear, for the future the past, for the ideal hero the perfect servant of God, for free-will fatalism.

Among Jewish sects the Hasaya especially were conspicuous as fatalists. Rabbi Jeshua has been depicted by modern writers as a Greek philosopher, a French poet, a German mystic, an English Christian; but in the rude chronicle of Simeon has Saddik, he is presented in his true character as a Hebrew fatalist and an Oriental prophet; and it is thus that, after clearing our minds from the influence of Western idiosyncrasies and modern thought, we should strive to regard him, according to the expressive hyperbole of the Hebrew tongue, as "the Slave of God."

CHAPTER VII.

THE DEATH OF RABBI JESHUA.

Savanarola—A parallel—The road to Jerusalem—The procession—Revolutionary acts—Conflict with the authorities—Presage of defeat—The Passover—The arrest—The trial—False accusation and condemnation—The popular revulsion—The execution—Burial of Rabbi Jeshua—The empty sepulchre.

ON the 23rd of May, 1498, being the vigil of the Ascension of St. Mark, the fierce and brutal Florentine crowd was gathered round the great cross-shaped gallows in the middle of the huge pile of faggots, where the bodies of the noble Savanarola and his two disciples were burning after their cruel execution in the great piazza of the city.

Tried as a false prophet but without evidence being found against him; silent under the accusations of his enemies; taunted by the rabble because no divine interposition saved him from his fate; tortured by his executioners, and his body finally carried away so that no tomb is now to be found covering his remains, the once venerated teacher of his ungrateful countrymen suffered the ignominious death which has testified ever since to the purity of his life. Among the sins of that proud and luxurious city none is recorded darker or more sad than the martyrdom of her patriotic preacher Savanarola.

A parallel between historic episodes of Oriental and Western history is as a rule unsatisfactory, because of the race contrast which has been touched on in the preceding chapter. Yet if we were to seek in Europe for a character somewhat reproducing that of Rabbi Jeshua we should probably find none which more closely approached it than that of the great Florentine reformer.

Commencing his career as a preacher of ascetic habits, inveighing against the corruption of the Church and the luxury of the rich, he went through his life in complete confidence of the heaven-sent nature of his mission. He claimed to be able to predict the future, and is said to have prophesied his own fate before the tide of popular feeling turned against him. His power over the masses was due to the austerity of his life. He inculcated obedience to the lawful commands of the Church, and his enemies were never able to convict him of heresy. His influence reached its greatest height in Florence immediately before his death, when the famous burning of the *Vanitá* was enthusiastically undertaken by the populace, at his command.

His fall was due to the overpowering strength of the great ecclesiastical system which he attacked, and to the enmity of the Roman pontiff, whom he nevertheless acknowledged as head of the Church. During his career he showed a marvellous power of persuading the lower classes; yet in the end a fearful revulsion of mob caprice ensured his doom, and the people whom he had loved and taught, and saved from gross sin and degradation, turned fiercely upon him with the savage cry, "His blood be upon us, and on our children."

These words which describe the career and the fate of Savanarola, might be applied almost without alteration to Rabbi Jeshua. Yet there was between them still the contrast of the two races to which they each belonged; for while Savanarola from a political aspect was distinguished as a successful statesman, Rabbi Jeshua's political programme was entirely summed up in his assumption of the character of the Messiah.

It was on Palm Sunday that Savanarola, in 1498, entered the gloomy prison whence he only went out again to his doom. It was on another Palm Sunday, more than fourteen centuries earlier, that

THE DEATH OF RABBI JESHUA.

Rabbi Jeshua first reached the fortress city where his cruel fate awaited him. By the white road which runs round the southern slope of chalky Olivet, the small band of Galilean pilgrims approached the Holy City. It was the lovely season of the Passover, when cool breezes, and blue skies dappled with fleecy clouds, prevailed over the "King's Mountain." The flowers of the field which Rabbi Jeshua loved, and from which he drew his glorious similes of faith and humility, were springing beside the path and clothing the dusty slopes. The red anemone, more beautiful than Solomon in all his glory, the great purple iris, the lily of the valleys, the white narcissus, the rose of Sharon, the blushing phloxes, coloured like the faint tint of the Eastern afterglow, which Rabbi Jeshua likened to the dawn of the kingdom of God, covered with a variegated carpet the stony Mount of Anointing, and hung in clusters over the gloomy valley of Gehenna. The breeze rustled through the dark olives of the garden of Gethshemen, sending waves of silver rippling through the groves, and in the silence of Eastern noon the distant hum of the crowded city was wafted across the deep ravine of Kidron.

It was from this white mountain path that the walls of Jerusalem first met the eyes of the band of the Hasaya as they halted at the turn of the descending road. The huge square façade of the Holy House, blazing with plates of gold, and hung with the gigantic vine bunches over the mystic veil, rose high above the marble colonnades of Herod's enclosure, and above the ancient ramparts of Solomon and Nehemiah. The great rock of Antonia, with its crenelated battlements, guarded the fane on the north. The domes of the houses, the narrow shady lanes, the hippodrome, the royal palaces, the synagogues, the great towers west of the town, the waving trees of Herod's garden, the white sepulchres to the north, the conspicuous monument of the kings of Judah: all these famous buildings, often described by travellers to the simple Galilean peasants, were now for the first time actually visible to their eyes, and it was with feelings of awe and admiration that they beheld the great stones of the Temple walls, the carved friezes of the sepulchral monuments, the impregnable citadel of the upper city. To the Roman or the Greek, fresh from the wondrous cities of his native land, the little town may have appeared mean and ugly, its architecture tasteless, its public works insignificant; but to the Galilean, who came from the mud huts of Capharnahum or the reed cabins of Jordan, such splendour indeed justified the enthusiasm of the Psalmist, even as the Land of Promise had of old appeared to the wanderers of the desert to be indeed a country flowing with milk and honey.

From the slope of Olivet the throngs within the Temple courts were plainly visible. The crowds of worshippers, the animals led to sacrifice, the bands of barefooted priests could be seen; and in the booths to the east beneath the cloisters the changers of money, and the sellers of sacrifices for the poor, had their recognised place outside the limit of that sacred court which no Gentile might enter.

It was the first day of the new year which was being celebrated. The great beacon was that night to be lighted on Olivet, to announce by a chain of bonfires to the exiles in Assyria the appearance of the new moon in Jerusalem. The witnesses crowded in the Beth Yenezek had been examined by the Sanhedrim, and had testified to the appearance of the slender crescent above their heads. The month had been pronounced sanctified, the great ram's-horns had been blown, the wood offering offered, the tender palm-spathes from the groves of Jericho were borne by the citizens in triumph.

The fame of Rabbi Jeshua had preceded him.

It was known that the Galilean prophet was on his way from Jericho, and the curious crowds awaited the arrival of the little procession with eagerness. The disciples sent on before pressed into the service of their weary master the first beast they found, and the simple claim, "for the service of God," was easily admitted by the devout owner.

In triumph, then, the Hasaya advanced to the city. The palms plucked in honour of the new year, destined to be laid upon the roof of the Temple cloisters, were borne in procession; the day of victory appeared at length to have dawned, and the fatalistic expectations of Rabbi Jeshua seemed on the eve of fulfilment.

There was nothing unusual in the approach of a pilgrim band at the Passover season singing psalms of pious triumph; nothing very alarming in the popular enthusiasm at first sight. But there were cries heard by priests and rulers as the crowd neared the gate, which foreboded a religious disturbance of most serious character.

In after days a parallel was drawn by the followers of Rabbi Jeshua between his entry and that of the promised Monarch, whom Zechariah had described as coming to the daughter of Zion "lowly and riding upon an ass," and the idea of a triumphal entry of the Messiah was present to their minds even on that day when first they approached Jerusalem.

Many among the Jewish crowd ventured to echo the cries of the Hasaya. They saluted Rabbi Jeshua by the title Son of David, which to them, but not to the Galileans, was synonymous with that of Messiah. They cast their garments (as men still do before Eastern kings) in his path, and thus, borne on the crest of that great wave of popular enthusiasm, Rabbi Jeshua entered the precincts of the Temple, followed by his zealous and fanatical disciples.

That this visit was the first which he had ever paid to the Jerusalem Temple is plain from the events which followed. The Hasaya, we know, neglected the ordinary ritual of sacrifice and worship, and we have no record of any annual visits paid by Rabbi Jeshua to Jerusalem whilst living in Galilee. The institution of regular booths, whereat the change for the Temple tax might be obtained and sacrifices bought, was a recognised part of the ritual. These shops were without the sacred court, in the cloisters of the Gentiles; they were recognised by the Sanhedrim, and excited no feeling of surprise among the worshippers. To the Galileans, however, the institution of a cattle-market within the Holy Mountain appeared no less than a desecration of the Temple; and in the tumult of religious excitement, which had arisen with the suddenness that characterises all popular movements in the East, the fury of the mob, directed by the zeal of the great puritan prophet, was spent on the unhappy traders who bartered their wares in Solomon's Porch.

It was thus that the popular excitement assuaged itself. The triumph was at its height, and the burning of the *Vanità* by the Florentine mob, at the bidding of Savanarola, is the only fitting parallel to the scene which took place on Rabbi Jeshua's entry into the Temple. But, like Savanarola, his trial and death followed hard on the moment of his greatest popularity.

The booths were torn down, the dove-coops tossed over the walls, the unhappy dealers, scourged and bleeding, were driven out of the Temple gates. But the Hasaya went no further in their zeal; they took no part in the services of the sanctuary, and they left the worshippers undisturbed in the inner courts. Having gazed with awe and admiration on the Holy House, they retreated from the enclosure; the outburst of popular fury subsided, the crowd dispersed, and with evening Rabbi Jeshua retired to rest in the cool shadow of the olive groves, under the pale radiance of the Passover crescent.

Thus, then, the moment of triumph passed away, for the expectations of the Hasaya were doomed to disappointment. The popular enthusiasm placed in the hands of Rabbi Jeshua a power which a vulgar revolutionist might have employed for his own advancement, but which to a fatalist devoutly awaiting the interference of supernatural authority was a sign of the great catastrophe, to be watched and followed, rather than a force to be guided and utilised. Perhaps in the first heat of the popular fury the Roman tyranny and the sacerdotal power might have been, at least for a time, overthrown; but Rabbi Jeshua paused to debate and argue while the mob demanded a leader, and thus incurred the fate which ever awaits the idol of the populace when once the fickle affection of the crowd is diverted in a new direction.

The emergency appears to have been met by the priestly party with presence of mind and consummate tact. To acknowledge a Messiah neither born at Bethlehem nor descended from David, a peasant of Galilee belonging to a sect of doubtful orthodoxy, was so plainly contrary to the whole system of traditional exegesis on which the very idea of the Anointed King was based, that it could have never for a moment occurred to the educated Jews that the populace were right in their impulsive acceptance of the newly arrived claimant. And we may also perhaps doubt whether those in power would have found themselves ready to accept even a Messiah of indisputable pretensions when actually appearing among them, however sincere might be their aspirations for the kingdom of God, while yet remaining an object of pious desire in the dim future of a theoretical millennium.

The Sanhedrim resolved therefore to treat the new prophet as a "refractory elder" inculcating heretical doctrines without due authority—an offence for which, if the Rabbi should persist in his contumacy, the legal punishment was death by strangling at Jerusalem and on a holiday. It was, however, a matter of no little delicacy to undertake, for two reasons. First, that the love of the peasantry of Galilee had to a certain extent recommended Rabbi Jeshua to the turbulent mob of Jerusalem. Secondly, because, however bold and original may have been the character of his doctrine, it could not easily be shown to have been at variance with either the spirit or the letter of the Law. When first the question was asked by the priests by what authority Rabbi Jeshua taught, his answer was in the highest degree embarrassing, for while announcing himself a disciple of the venerated Hanan, he also boldly intimated, by a fable of unmistakable meaning, his opinion that the days of the existing hierarchy were numbered, and that the care of the vineyard was about to be taken from them, and given to those more faithful husbandmen who were represented by the sect of the Hasaya.

The pride which thus rebelled against the power of priests and rulers was not however sufficient to blind the great Rabbi to a recognition of his actual defeat. He saw that the popular excitement had collapsed as quickly as it had grown; he knew that suffering and death awaited the unsuccessful revolutionist, unless indeed the hand of God should suddenly intervene.

On the slope of Olivet he sat gazing sadly at the unfriendly city where his enemies already plotted against his life, and sadly answered his pupils as they praised the magnificence of the great tawny ramparts which crowned the opposite hill.

It may be that the words which Rabbi Simeon here puts in the Master's mouth are not historical. It may well be thought that they are coloured by the remembrance of that great catastrophe which, still in the future when Rabbi Jeshua spoke, had befallen the fated city ere his words were recorded.

Nevertheless, there is nothing in the imputed prediction which differs from the ordinary language of apocalyptic literature of a period earlier than that of Rabbi Jeshua's career. The expectation of a time of national disgrace and sorrow; the influence of the latest work in Jewish sacred literature, the so-called book of Daniel; the belief that in neglecting to recognise his claims as the Messiah the Jews had only fulfilled the spirit of prophecies which crowded to his memory, would sufficiently account for the gloomy forebodings which Rabbi Jeshua imparted to his followers.

Meanwhile a fortnight elapsed and the Passover-eve arrived. The Hasaya, who, if Josephus may be credited, were excluded from the Temple court, took no part in the ritual of the day; but the evening feast commemorative of the Exodus—the lamb, the bitter herbs, and the cup of blessing—constituted a family festivity which was celebrated by Rabbi Jeshua and his followers in common with the rest of the nation.

On that fatal evening the opportunity long awaited by his enemies arrived. The Jewish worshippers were engaged until a late hour in the Temple service, and after the Paschal Supper they indulged in feasting in their houses; for the Mishna expressly notes that although only four cups of wine were recognised in connection with the ceremony, yet between the second and the third a Jew might drink as many as he wished, and from other passages we may gather that excess was not uncommon among the feasters. So long indeed was the supper protracted that many used to fall asleep before it was ended.

The inhabitants of the city being thus occupied in their houses the streets of Jerusalem were no longer filled with the excited and turbulent throngs of pilgrims whose enthusiasm had threatened to prove a danger to the established order of sacerdotal rule. No more fitting opportunity could be expected for the apprehension of the leader who might it was feared yet accomplish his threat of overturning the Saducean party. The traitor had been found, the movements of Rabbi Jeshua had been watched, and the arrest was quietly and quickly effected.

In the dim shadows of the dusky garden of Gethshemen the Hasaya pilgrims lay curled in their rough mantles, sleeping in the balmy night air of the Eastern spring. The houses of the city were full to overflowing, and the love of solitude, of freedom, and of the open country natural to the hermits of the Galilean deserts, led forth the great Rabbi and his disciples to the cool retreat of the olive groves. It was here that their rest was broken by the lurid light of the torches, gleaming on the bronze helmets of the Roman auxiliaries, and on the scimetars of the servants of Joseph the high priest. But little resistance was offered, for it was a principle of the Hasaya to be obedient to actual authority, and Rabbi Jeshua was, moreover, conscious of the irreproachable orthodoxy of all his doctrines. Thus, with the same fatalistic resignation which marks his whole career, he surrendered himself, with the bitter taunt, "Why was I not taken teaching in the Temple in the sight and hearing of all men?"

The Sanhedrim had been lately expelled from the "chamber of hewn stone" by the Roman governor, and the examination of the refractory elder was therefore no longer conducted within the precincts of the Holy House, but in the palace of the high priest in the city. It was thither that Rabbi Jeshua was conducted, and it was there that he was formally interrogated as to his doctrines. In the cold dark hours of the early spring dawn the examination was commenced, and beside the brazier in the outer hall the faithful Simeon—the future chronicler—sat among the menials of the great house and heard the voice of the Temple crier ("the cock," as he was called) proclaim the dawn, sadly recalling the sad presage of his master that before that dawn broke he would be forsaken and betrayed.

That the Sadducean party were actuated by political rather than religious motives in the arrest and trial of Rabbi Jeshua; that he was indeed, like Savanarola, the victim of society, and the vanquished opponent of an established government, is sufficiently clear from the simple narrative of Simeon; but it is perhaps less certain whether the final condemnation of the prisoner was due, as in Savanarola's case, to fierce hatred and unscrupulous falsification of evidence, or whether it resulted from a sincere though mistaken and fanatical belief in the heretical criminality of the victim.

The charge of false doctrines appears to have entirely broken down, and the trial turned finally on the pretensions of Rabbi Jeshua to the office and dignity of Messiah. The high priest demanded categorically an answer from Rabbi Jeshua on this point. "Art thou Messiah, the Son of the Holy One, blessed be He?" demanded Joseph. And the answer was equally definite, though to it Rabbi Jeshua added a quotation from the book of Daniel, which illustrated his views as to the career of the Son of God.

It is astonishing to read that for this answer Rabbi Jeshua was condemned as a blasphemer. There was nothing blasphemous in the assertion that he was Messiah, nor was the title "Son of God" connected in those days with any claim of a supernatural character. Every son of Israel was a son of God, and Messiah, pre-eminently, was called by this title in the Psalms. Blasphemy among the Jews consisted, as has already been pointed out, in the utterance of the Divine Name, and the Mishna states clearly that the blasphemer was not guilty until he expressed the Name, "which, when the judges heard, they were instructed to stand up and rend their garments, which might never again be sewn."

How, then, are we to understand the fact that after the simple answer "I am" had been given by the prisoner, the high priest arose at once and called the Sanhedrim to witness, by the rending of his garments, that the Divine Name had been uttered, the pronunciation of which, according to its letters, condemned the prisoner to death? There is only one explanation possible, and this we find in reading the chronicle in Hebrew: for the word "I am" was the ancient and original form of the Holy Name, by which Jehovah Himself had made Himself known to Moses.

With hateful cunning the high priest placed on the words with which Rabbi Jeshua naturally answered the direct question, perhaps asked with that very object, a construction which must have appeared plainly unjust to every person present. He declared that the Divine Name had been spoken, when only an affirmative answer of the same sound had been given ; and on this malicious and arbitrary decision the death-doom of Rabbi Jeshua, whom the assembled Sanhedrim had been unable to find guilty in any other matter, was cruelly pronounced. In the history of priestly tyranny among the Jews, there was perhaps no blacker stain than the sacrifice of the innocent victim whom the Sadducees thus ruthlessly and falsely condemned, in order to save their own authority, and to satisfy their long-nursed hatred and thirst for vengeance.

This decision summarily dispensed with all cause for further inquiry, and but one bar remained to be removed in order that the unjust sentence might be carried into effect—namely, the consent of the Roman governor, in whose hands alone the power of life and death was then vested. This, however, would be easily obtained. The cynical Roman knew little of the intricacies of Hebrew law, and cared little for the life of any Jew who appeared likely to raise a riot in the city. Once convinced that the liberation of this obscure prisoner might lead to revolution, the Procurator might, they argued, without any difficulty, be induced to authorise the execution.

The Procurator, however, had been well advised of the state of the case, and was aware that the condemnation of Rabbi Jeshua had resulted from sectarian hatred, and was probably not justified by any actual crime. He knew also that the populace had, only a few days before, received the Rabbi with every expression of enthusiastic delight; and with a sense of humanity and justice which contrasted with the blind and determined tyranny of the Sadducees, he placed the decision of the case in the hands of the people.

Astonishing, indeed, must have been the discovery which the Procurator then made of the sudden revulsion of feeling which was evinced by the savage cries of the mob demanding the death of their former favourite. Yet to those who knew the cause—so powerful to the Jewish mind, so ill-understood by the foreign ruler—there is but little difficulty in explaining the change.

The rumour of what had occurred in the high

priest's palace had no doubt spread rapidly, and had been magnified and distorted by repetition, and perhaps purposely exaggerated by the priestly party for their own ends. Rabbi Jeshua, it was asserted, had blasphemed wilfully in the presence of the Sanhedrim. He had perhaps endeavoured to employ magic arts, and to bewitch the council by invocation of the Name through which all incantations were rendered effective. The old accusations which had been brought against him by the Pharisees were revived, and the populace—unlike the Galilean peasantry—was not acquainted with the unfailing goodness and gentleness of character, with the piety and love which were known, by his own fellow-countrymen and followers, to distinguish the great teacher.

Had these events taken place in Galilee, the peasantry might have risen to protect the man who loved them and whom they almost worshipped. In Jerusalem, on the other hand, he was a stranger among strangers, a new teacher among men long accustomed to be led and guided by the priestly party whom he had defied. The false accusation which in his own land would have appeared incredible, was easily believed by the mob of Jerusalem; and the plea on which he was condemned proved to be one easily grasped by the multitude, and constituting, when vouched for by respected authority, a full and sufficient reason for the condemnation of the Galilean Messiah.

The Roman Procurator yielded at once to the unexpected expression of the popular will. He had had sad experience of the turbulence of his subjects in questions connected with their religious beliefs. He had done his best to save the life of an innocent man, but it was better that one Jew should perish—even if innocent—than that the Roman governor should find himself in conflict with the whole nation, at a time when his inability to rule his district was already drawing unwelcome attention upon him from Italy, and threatened to result in his final disgrace and the loss of a lucrative post. Thus, by the people whom he had loved, by the very class for whom he had toiled and taught, by the peasantry whom he alone had deemed worthy of care and guidance, the fate of the great Rabbi was sealed, and the doom of the rejected leader was pronounced without remorse.

The barbarous cruelty of the recognised methods of Jewish execution was, no doubt, one among many reasons which justified the more civilised Romans in forbidding the infliction of the death penalty by order of the Sanhedrim. Four capital punishments were recognised by Jewish law, namely stoning, burning, beheading, and strangling. Stoning was effected by first throwing the criminal over a precipice some ten feet in height, and then by casting a single stone on his body. If this failed of its object, the whole assembled crowd was allowed to complete the barbarous deed, and the body of the victim was afterwards crucified until sundown.

By burning was intended, not the death at the stake, which had originally been sanctioned by custom, but a method of execution so ingeniously cruel as to be worthy of the Chinese themselves. The criminal was strangled by two men while a lighted taper was thrust into his mouth, unless, indeed, death was caused immediately by suffocation.

By beheading was intended either execution with an axe or execution with a sword. By strangulation was understood the same punishment as burning, but without the additional torture of the lighted taper.

By such refined methods of execution, the Jews were wont to punish those accused of idolatry, witchcraft, profanation of the sabbath, or any other capital crime of which superstitious witnesses might accuse the victim before a senate of fanatical, superstitious, and sometimes corrupt judges.

As a rebellious elder, or as a false peophet, Rabbi Jeshua might have been put to death by strangling; as a blasphemer he should have been stoned, according to Jewish law; as an offender against the public peace, he was crucified by the Romans, after the customary scourging which usually preceded this mode of execution. Thus, though balked of the cruel satisfaction of despatching their victim by the slow and uncertain method of a characteristic Oriental execution, the Jews at least saw accomplished the disgraceful punishment which, according to the law, was specially accursed, and which formed the ordinary sequel of the blasphemer's death.

So rapidly did the trial, the condemnation, and the execution follow one upon the other, that it was only the third hour after sunrise when Rabbi Jeshua was nailed to the cross by the native auxiliaries, on whom—and not on the noble legionaries of Italy—is to be laid the disgrace of having insulted and illtreated the patient victim of Jewish fanaticism and sectarian hate. The bitter drink which the charity of the great ladies of Jerusalem provided for criminals was refused by Rabbi Jeshua. The arrangement of signals, by which, even at the moment of execution, the trial might be resumed, and punishment suspended, on the arrival of a fresh witness, was not used in this case, because the alleged offence had been committed in presence of the very judges themselves. There was thus no mitigation of the terrors and suffering of the execution, and no respite given before the hurried accomplishment of an unjust sentence.

Round the rocky knoll which rose beside the stony lane outside the city wall, the fierce mob of the Passover pilgrims was gathered. The curses of the multitude greeted their idol of yesterday; the bitter exclamation of despair which escaped the dying Rabbi was misinterpreted into a vain appeal to the intervention of the mysterious Elias; and like Savanarola, Rabbi Jeshua was taunted with his inability to escape his doom, and because no miraculous intervention of Providence saved him from his fate.

Along the sides of the barren hillock, on the battlements of the dark city rampart, the crowds swarmed and struggled. The white robes of the priests might be seen lining the Temple walls; the armour of the Roman guard gleamed from the fortress of Antonia. The golden plates of the great Temple glittered in the sunlight; the thin veil of the far-off precipices of Moab stretched purple in the distance. The blue sky flecked with white clouds, the fresh breeze from the sea which stirred the olive groves, the gay carpet of green which half hid the white slopes of Olivet, all spoke of the new-born life of the glorious spring to the sufferer whose days in this world were well-nigh done.

The green corn was high on Olivet, but the harvest which Rabbi Jeshua had hoped to gather had vanished away. The purple lilies on that bare hill-top, stamped under foot by the crowd, were fit emblems no longer of the glory of Solomon, but rather of the downfall of that eagerly desired kingdom which, but a few hours ago, had appeared to be bursting forth into bloom. The white wings of the stork-pilgrims wending their way to the rich plains of Kinnereth, to the marshes of Jordan, to the meadows of Galilee, on which Rabbi Jeshua might never again hope to look, clove the blue heaven above his head; but no angel hosts came down to deliver the rejected Messiah; no miraculous interposition rescued Rabbi Jeshua from his doom; for to him was allotted, through the terrors of martyrdom, an undying fame, destined to spread from East to West across the world, and a glory far surpassing the lesser honours of a merely Jewish Messiah.

To us who regard that scene by the light of later events, the swelling hills outside the city walls are seen bristling not merely with the three crosses of that fatal day, but with the innumerable bodies of crucified Jews whom the Roman legionaries of Titus, in grim jest, grouped along the line of the stubborn ramparts of the beleaguered city, until there was no longer room for the crosses, nor crosses for the bodies. If there was one crime which more than another brought vengeance on the doomed city of Jerusalem, surely it was this one of the unjust death of the Great Man of the nation; and in the crucifixion of the very populace which had crucified its Messiah, we mark an historical instance of grim poetic justice such as is rarely afforded by the irony of fate.

There is but little to add to the history of the failure and untimely termination of Rabbi Jeshua's short career.

His body, according to the usual Jewish custom, should have been cast into the common sepulchre of criminals near the city; but from such degradation it was rescued through the influence of a rich Pharisee, who buried it in his own rock sepulchre, among the gardens outside the town. Here it was reverently laid by the few friends who had remained faithful, and the great stone cylinder was rolled before the narrow entrance ere the eve of the Sabbath had commenced.

But, like Savanarola, Rabbi Jeshua was fated to leave not even a relic of his mortality. The women who came to embalm his body found the tomb broken open, the body no longer within. The stone had been rolled away, and the vanishing figure of a white-robed stranger was seen, or believed to be seen, by the terrified and dismayed mourners, who fled forthwith from the sepulchre.

Many were the legends which arose in consequence of this mysterious sequel to the history of the great Rabbi; but the chronicle of Simeon has Saddik closes with the account of the open tomb and the trembling women; and of Rabbi Jeshua, as of Moses, it may truly be said that "no man knoweth his sepulchre unto this day."

CHAPTER VIII.

LEGENDARY HISTORY.

The desert—Satyrs and the Lilith—Jewish demonology—Cabbalistic Trinity—The Syrian pantheon—The death of Tammuz—Legends of Rabbi Jeshua—Legendary histories of the Jews—The concealment of Messiah—Persecution of the Hasaya—Phahil—Philo's description of the Hasaya—They become extinct.

FEW save those who know by experience can conceive the oppression which is caused by the sense of solitude in the desert.

The silence which is due to the absence of life and of vegetation becomes a burden to the ear accustomed to the bustle of cities and to the rustling of the wind in the trees. The broad plains, the mighty precipices, the fantastic peaks and ridges, present a terrible and unfriendly aspect. The cry of the eagle re-echoes from the hard rocks, and the ghostly herds of the wild goats flit past in the distance with noiseless swiftness. The loneliness of the wilderness strikes even the stoutest heart with a feeling of danger and uncertainty, and the nerves are strung by the dry atmosphere to an unnatural and painful tension.

What wonder, then, that the desert should have been peopled from the earliest ages with doleful creatures, or that terrible forms should still be believed by the Arab wanderers to haunt the untrodden wastes.

Among the crumbling ruins of the wilderness, the Hebrew prophet conjures up in imagination a ghostly band of obscene demons.

"And thorns shall come up in her palaces, nettles and brambles in the fortresses thereof, and it shall be an abode of serpents, and a stable for the ostrich. The jackals of the desert shall meet with the wild beast of the shores, the satyr shall cry to his fellow, and Lilith shall find rest there." So does the poet describe the desolation of the southern deserts; and in like manner of Babylon he predicts, "Their houses shall be full of doleful creatures, the ostriches shall dwell there, and the satyrs shall dance there."

In these and other passages of the Old Testament we find expressed the universal superstition of Semitic races peopling the solitude with phantom forms of evil spirits.

Even in the constitutions of the Law of Moses

some of these superstitions are incorporated, just as Mohammed, when preaching the second monotheistic creed of the Semitic races, also incorporated in his ritual some of the observances which belonged to the "time of ignorance" before Islam.

Thus Azazel, to whom the scapegoat was annually devoted, was the prince of demons, well known in Syrian and Arab mythology, and his appropriate habitation was in the wilderness. The worship of the satyrs, or "hairy demons," was expressly forbidden by Moses; but their existence was not the less credited, and Ashima, the later Asmodeus, the Persian Ashma Daevo, was a deity personified by a goat, and partook in all respects, as evidenced by the story of Sara, daughter of Raguel, as well as by the legend of his attack on the harem of Solomon, of the traditional nature of the satyr.

The Lilith, or female demon, the succuba of the Jews, the lamia who carried away and devoured new-born infants, was a yet more terrible creation of the imagination. She also was a dweller in the desert, and the ascetics who lived in the wilderness were supposed to be specially subject to her nocturnal assaults. Of the Liliuth were thus born evil demons, the Hengeh who leapt out on unwary travellers. Lilith was one of the four evil wives of

Sammael the prince of demons, and she appears as the temptress of Adam not less than the enemy of his sons.

It must not be forgotten that however pure the Judaism of the time of Rabbi Jeshua may have been, the superstitions of earlier ages were still firmly credited by the nation at large. The common beliefs of the peasantry find expression more than once in the chronicle of Simeon has Saddik, and the mythology of Syria even tinged the belief of Rabbi Jeshua's disciples within a century of his death.

More than one mythological system was known to the Jews, and from each in turn they derived some portion of the innumerable superstitions in which they believed. There were ancient Accadian legends which the patriarchs had brought from beyond Euphrates; there were the astronomical and phallic worships of the Canaanites; and the kindred myths of the Phœnicians and the Syrians. There was the great Hittite Pantheon, and there was the complex system of Egyptian theology. Against these the Law testified, yet were the gross and cruel rites of Ashtoreth and Moloch never entirely abandoned before the Captivity; and though the influence of Egypt appears to have been at first very week, it is thought by some authors that in the mystic Urim we have an echo of an Egyptian method of divination.

But it was during the period of the Captivity, under the Persian influence, that the mythology of the Jews first became more fully developed. They themselves in poetic language acknowledged that they had learned the names of the angels in Babylon, and in Babylon no less their demonology was created.

"If we could see the evil demons," said one rabbi, "no creature might stand before them." The crowding in the synagogue is because of them, bruises on the legs are their doing, and the shabbiness of clothes. The claws of demons may be seen in the dust in the morning, and the powdered skin of a black kitten anointing the eyes will make them visible.

That man might be possessed by such evil spirits was a common belief. The maniac dwelling in the rock tombs of the desert was considered to be their prey; and if a man be bitten by a dog he must drink only through a brass tube for twelve months, lest he see the phantom form of Kanti Klurus, the demon of hydrophobia.

No less general was the belief in sorcery, divination, witchcraft, and necromancy, in astrology and the charming of serpents, in the power of controlling the fall of rain which some wizards possessed, in the foretelling of the future by the fall of arrows, or by conjunctions of the planets.

In the mythology of the Assyrians, and in the dualism of the Persian faith, we find the main elements of the later Jewish superstition. The solemn cherubs, or " strong bulls," of Assyria with their great wings and grave bearded faces; the messengers, or angels of the chief divinities, the fiery disks with which Marduk was armed, find a place in Hebrew poetry no less than the snake-like Devil and the evil genii of the Persian Zoroastrian faith.

From the Egyptian school the Hasaya also borrowed some of the mystic dogmas of the Cabbala. Among the Alexandrines the whole pantheon of good and evil spirits was marshalled under the opposing powers, Sar-Happanim the Angel of the Presence, and Sammael the Prince of the Powers of the Air. Cabbalists were found at a later period among the disciples of Rabbi Jeshua, and in their works we trace the foreign doctrines of Judeo-Alexandrine philosophy: the Light shining in darkness which cannot comprehend or enclose it; the trinity of Metatron—the Angel of the Presence—Logos, the Word or Wisdom, by whom all things were made, and Adam Kadmon, the old

Adam, the firstborn son of God. The deification of their great teacher was carried to such an extent that his Cabbalistic disciples did not scruple to identify him with an actual incarnation of the Logos, an idea so foreign to the whole spirit of Rabbi Jeshua's original teaching, that we may even suppose him to have been entirely ignorant of the existence of teachers who elaborated such mystic dogmas.

Unchecked by the authority of the Sanhedrim and the puritan zeal of the devout, the old mythology of Iran flourished in the north of Palestine and in Syria proper at the time of which we are treating. Surrounded by a host of genii and demons, the great astronomical deities were universally worshipped under various names. Baal Ishtar or Jupiter, Ashtoreth or Venus his consort, Hadad, Rimmon, Tammuz or Adonis, the offspring of the divine pair, formed the trinity of the Father God, the Mother of God, and the only Son, who was sacrificed to the wrath of the elder divinity, and again raised from the dead. In the death of Tammuz the nation annually mourned the approach of winter; in the joyful exclamation of his priests, who, on the 25th of December, used to proclaim, "Behold the virgin hath borne a son!" they welcomed the return of spring. The festival of flowers was celebrated—as it has perhaps always been since man and flowers were created—in the joyful Easter time. The fiery sacrifice of children, typical of the destruction of Tammuz, and the licentious mysteries of Ashtoreth symbolising the fruitfulness of the great creation, were rites which, however disgusting and unnatural they may now appear to our more refined minds, are nevertheless to be found celebrated among the peasantry of Christian lands even in the nineteenth century.

Nor is the ancient worship of Asia even now extinct, though idolatry has been scourged by Islam since the time of Rabbi Jeshua. In the fourth century the Venus of Ascalon was still worshipped, and Marnas, the Jupiter of Gaza, had a temple standing. In Bethlehem the mourning of Tammuz was not forgotten; in Accho the sacred baths of Ashtoreth were still frequented. Sacred trees condemned by the Sanhedrim were nevertheless still consecrated to the Assyrian Asherah, the goddess of fertility; stone heaps were gathered in honour of Mercury, and the stone worship and mountain worship of a remote period were preserved, with rites of a licentious character, which are still practised in Lebanon.

The great genii of Persia, the demon of the whirlwind, the satyr of the desert, the foul ghoul who has superseded the beautiful demon Lilith, the goat-fiends of the wilderness, and the goblins and phantoms of ruins and caverns, are beings of whose existence the wandering Bedawi and the Syrian peasant are still most devoutly convinced; while the belief in magic, in snake-charming, in possession, and in incarnations of supernatural powers are still as vivid and real as of old.

It is not without an object that the superstitions of Syria have thus been briefly described. The chronicle of which we have hitherto followed the general outline contains many marvellous stories, which are more or less directly connected with the beliefs of the age; and it is important to keep clearly in view, in treating this part of the subject, the fact that the peasant chronicler was not less influenced by the superstitions of the day than were the peasants among whom Rabbi Jeshua lived; while a correct appreciation of the origin and meaning of the Phœnician myths and Alexandrine philosophy renders it more easy to comprehend the growth of that legendary history which gradually grew up in connection with the true facts of the life of Rabbi Jeshua, which were obscured and finally altogether lost beneath the overgrowth of a semi-pagan mysticism which culminated in his deification.

We have already seen that Rabbi Simeon believed in the desert demons, whom he represents as assaulting Rabbi Jeshua during the period of his hermit life in the wilderness. We have already noted how the maniacs and nervous patients whom the physician soothed or healed are represented by the simple chronicler as possessed by devils. We should therefore be prepared for the relation of other wonders by a writer so imbued with the spirit of the times, so credulous of the marvellous, so ignorant of any science or art.

It is observable, however, that the number of legends, and the detail with which they are circumstantiated increases as the date of the various chronicles recedes from the contemporary to the later period. Rabbi Jeshua's birth and early years are not recorded by Simeon, but more than one discordant account exists, clothed in a legendary garb, and surrounded by supernatural phenomena.

This, indeed, is a peculiarity constantly observable in Hebrew literature. The history of Jewish heroes remained for a time unwritten, and was handed down from generation to generation by oral tradition. Thus, when finally committed to writing, it included the legends with which a marvel-loving people had gradually surrounded the historic narrative, and the more remote the period which elapsed before the chronicle was actually composed the more stupendous and circumstantial the miracles which were therein incorporated. As an instance, we may indicate the first and second books of the Maccabees, representing the contrast between an actual history and a legendary account of the same facts. In the sober narrative of the first no mention of any marvellous occurrences is found. In the elaborate but inaccurate romance written later, a supernatural machinery is freely employed, mysterious phantoms appear in every page, visions and prophetic dreams precede each great event. It is not often in Jewish literature that we have so favourable an opportunity of distinguishing between the solid facts of an historical episode and the mythical overgrowth which has obscured and surrounded them.

It can scarcely be doubted that many of the marvellous circumstances which are chronicled by the later biographers of Rabbi Jeshua, owe their origin to the apologetic character of the various essays, which aim at demonstrating the complete fulfilment, in his life and actions, of all that could have been expected of the Jewish Messiah; but in the case of Rabbi Simeon this bias is less remarkable, and we have, as a rule, only to take into account the very late period of his life at which his recollections were written down by one of his friends. If, during the lifetime of Rabbi Jeshua, marvellous stories had already been circulated concerning his powers we may feel sure that they did not cease with his death. The memory of his peasant disciples, prone to exaggeration and to a love of wonder, must have magnified many occurrences which, had they been described by an educated and impartial eye-witness, would have seemed natural enough.

The marvels related in connection with the life of Rabbi Jeshua bear a close affinity to the miracles which are attributed in the Hebrew Scriptures to the great prophets of an earlier period, to Moses, Elijah, or Elisha. Like the latter, he is said to have raised the dead and fed the multitude with miraculous food. Like Moses or Elijah, to have passed through the waters dryshod. He was believed to possess the power of controlling the winds and storms, as Elijah of old was said to have brought rain, and as the dervish of our own times is firmly believed to be capable of smiting with drought an ungrateful country.

But perhaps the most curious of these legends is that of the vision which is said to have been seen by the two companions of Rabbi Jeshua, one of whom was Simeon himself, during his retreat to the heights of Hermon, where the Druse candidates for initiation still make periodical gatherings. Elias, the forerunner, and Moses, who also according to some was to precede Messiah, are said to have here appeared and talked with Rabbi Jeshua; but we are left to wonder whether the identification of these mysterious visitants was due to the imagination of the disciple, or in what degree the vision was accredited by the Rabbi himself.

At a period so remote, and with materials so scanty, it is impossible to judge what the foundation on which such legends were based may have been. We are of course at liberty entirely to discredit them, or to see in them the interpolations of a later copyist; but when we consider the superstitious reverence with which Rabbi Jeshua was regarded, the universal belief in the everyday occurrence of miracles held by the ignorant peasantry of Palestine, the length of time which elapsed before the recollections of Simeon were written down, the desire to vindicate the Messiahship of their Master which was so intensely felt by the disappointed Hasaya, it is perhaps a better view that the wondrous legends which so rapidly sprung up had their origin in deeds which were not understood by the original witnesses, and the true character of which has been hopelessly obscured by the repetition at a later period of their confused memories of facts.

The circumstances of the death and burial of Rabbi Jeshua were peculiarly adapted to the fabrication of such legends. The Semitic mind is characterised by a tenacity which prevents the eradication of an idea, once firmly grasped, from being affected even by the rudest shock of the most abrupt disillusion. Thus, when the sorrowing friends who had loved the great Rabbi beheld his shameful death they were yet unable to grasp the fact that their hopes were at an end, and their hero departed. They hoped daily and hourly against hope for his return. In despondency and grief, they still remembered his predictions of a great trouble which must precede his triumph. They expected still the supernatural revolution which should inaugurate the reign of Messiah.

It was during the first days of this period of expectation, that they heard of the deserted tomb and the mysterious disappearance of the body of Rabbi Jeshua. There is no evidence in the chronicle of Simeon that any of the immediate followers of the Rabbi ever again beheld him in life or in death. They believed indeed the story of the frightened women perhaps more implicitly than we are justified in doing, considering the fact that

Oriental women have always been, and still are, the chief authors of marvellous tales. They were fully prepared to suppose that a period of concealment was necessary to the career of a Messiah whose triumph was yet to come, and they read with a new meaning the chapter of Isaiah's prophecy which they supposed to refer to the execution of their Master.

It was thus that the legends which are recorded of the reappearance of Rabbi Jeshua after death sprang up among his simple-minded, devoted, and grief-stricken friends: legends of his return to life, of his being caught up like Enoch or Elijah into the heavens, there to be concealed for a time until his hour should come. Such legends, however, are stamped as unauthentic by two circumstances: first, that they are not recorded in the original text of the chronicle of Rabbi Simeon; secondly, that the various versions which exist in other works are mutually inconsistent and contradictory.

The Hasaya then remained expectant even after their Master's death of his approaching return and final triumph. They still continued even to make converts for a time, and to inculcate so far as they understood them the doctrines of Rabbi Jeshua. Within thirty years of his murder, the Sanhedrim, usurping the right of execution during an interregnum of procurators, caused Jacob, the brother of Rabbi Jeshua, and others of the sect to be stoned as breakers of the Law. It was no doubt after this persecution that the Hasaya retreated to the district of Bethania beyond Jordan, and to the village of Phahil on the brink of the Jordan valley.

It was here, within the lifetime of Simeon has Saddik, that they remained in safety while the armies of Rome devastated Judea, and when the doomed city was at length surrounded by the girdle of the investing wall. The rumours of these troubles reached the peaceful pietists in their Perean retreat, and in the horrors of that siege they saw not so much the divine vengeance on the murderers of their Master, as the great period of trouble including the destruction of Jerusalem and the slaughter of Israel; the triumph of the Goim predicted by the prophets which was to precede the immediate return of Rabbi Jeshua as the Messiah triumphant.

Of the character of the sect in their retreat at Phahil we may gather some idea from the account which Philo has given of their life.

"They serve God," he writes, "with great piety, not in offering sacrifices but in self-sanctification.

They dwell in villages, and fly from cities because of the general immorality of their inhabitants, knowing that by contact therewith the soul is stricken with incurable ill, like the sickness which is due to a poisonous air.

"Some till the earth, others follow peaceful arts, and each works for himself and for his neighbour. They gather neither silver nor gold, nor seek to get riches by buying broad lands. Their care only is to gain the necessaries of life; and alone almost of all men they are without money or goods, rather through custom than because fortune has failed them, and they are deemed rich because to them riches are found in frugality and content. You will not find among them any maker of arrows, darts, swords, or helmets, of breastplates or bucklers, or of any armour, nor any who makes weapons of war, or who follows any trade that is hurtful. They know not at all the trades of merchants, of tavern-keepers, or of carriers, for they reject all that causes covetousness. There are no slaves among them, all are free, and work one for the other.

"They reject tyranny, not only as unjust and destructive of liberty, but even as impious, in changing the law of nature, which like a mother has nourished all men, and made them equal as brethren, not in name but in deed; whereas crafty covetousness has produced strangeness for friendship, and hate for love. The logic of philosophy being unneeded for virtue, they leave to the hunters of words; the physical sciences being beyond human understanding, to those who pretend to rise to the heavens; always excepting that which belongs to a belief in the existence of God, and the origin of all things that are. But morality they study with great zeal, taking for their guide the national law, the understanding of which they say is impossible for the human mind unaided by divine inspiration. They learn in this law at all times, but especially on the seventh day, which they hold sacred, and during which they cease from all other things. Gathered in the holy houses which they call synagogues, they form a congregation seated in ranks in suitable order, the young behind the aged. One takes the Holy Books and reads, another from among the more experienced expounds the difficult passages; for most doctrines among them, as among the ancients, are expressed in fables."

Such, then, was the simple and quiet life of these primitive pietists, awaiting in a condition of society only possible to an agricultural class the return of their Messiah.

The world rolled on, and the Hasaya were forgotten. The Alexandrine philosophers clamoured and disputed on the minutiæ of their allegorical interpretations. The mythologists of Asia Minor elaborated their symbolic teaching of native worship, and adored the trinity which men had believed in for thousands of years. Slowly and surely the systems of pagan theology crumbled and were frittered away. Christianity was spread by its zealous apostles along the shores of the Mediterranean, and even in the heart of imperial Rome. The heresy of the Docetes and of the Manichæans, representing Christ as a phantom first appearing at Jordan and never truly incarnate; and the dogmas of fifty sects of Gnostics, derived originally from the Platonic philosophy of Egypt, flourished for two hundred years in Syria and the Levant, side by side with the Jewish Cabbalism. Time passed, and the edict of Constantine established the faith throughout the empire. Pagan persecution ceased, and the internecine strife of the great heresies commenced. The dogmas of the Church were fought out and decided by councils. The inspiration of the New Testament, the canon, the rites and government of the Church, the nature of the Trinity, were defined, as the fabric grew and spread; and during all this time the little Galilean sect hoped on in the seclusion of its unknown home.

In the fourth century they still claimed among their number descendants of the family of Rabbi Jeshua. They were branded as heretics, not any longer by the Jews, but by the Greek orthodox Christians who then ruled Palestine.

In the fierce onslaught of the early campaigns of Mohammed and of Omar, they were apparently overwhelmed; but for four centuries, at least, the slowly dwindling community lived peacefully and obscurely among the rich plateaux and deep gorges of Perea, awaiting the "day of the Lord," which should come as a thief in the night.

Yet Rabbi Jeshua came not. For his work in this world was done, and the influence of his life was not the less powerful on men because the seal of martyrdom closed the record of his mortal career.

CHAPTER IX.

ENGLAND AND RABBI JESHUA.

The search in the city—Sadducees—Pharisees—Philosophers—Epicureans—The poor—The lost child.

LIKE a dream of the past, the scenery of Palestine faded from my view: the calm lake, with its rugged cliffs and black lava-fields, its oleander bushes and shingly beach; the stony hills with their brushwood of dark mastic; the brown plains, the yellow sand dunes with graceful tufts of palm; and I found myself once more in the great grey smoky city, with a lowering sky, a dripping of rain, a crowd of careworn, sordidly-dressed, pale-faced men, hurrying hither and thither, in pursuit of gold.

Now we know that the religion of the Hebrews has formed the basis of our own; and that the student can disentangle the wonderful braid, and trace the various skeins which have been intertwined in the formation of our modern creeds. Therefore it seemed to me possible that, though distinguished by race, by religion, and by character, I might yet be able to trace among the dwellers in the great city some echoes of the noble teaching, some marks of influence of the life and genius of the great Galilean Rabbi.

On this search, then, I set out, and finding before me the open doors of a large plain edifice, apparently consecrated to some religious purpose, I entered, and found indeed a congregation assembled.

The interior of the building was bare and ugly, the walls whitewashed, the dingy windows filled with small panes of common glass. Rows of high wooden pews, of most comfortless shape, filled the interior, and a huge wooden edifice, in three stories, rose like a gigantic tulip of dark oak colour. From inside the tulip-cup the preacher addressed his audience, while above him hung suspended a heavy sounding-board, looking like an extinguisher about to fall on his head. The device by which this great cupola was supported might have been thought typical of the dogmas which it re-echoed, for two fluted Corinthian pillars rose behind the preacher and supported one side of the superstructure, while the rest, braced up by some hidden and most unmechanical contrivance, stood unsupported in the air, the two other pillars, which should have been placed opposite those actually existing, having been omitted as interfering with the preacher's freedom of action.

My attention was first directed to the congregation. The majority were women, but there was a fair proportion of elderly men, and a few mild-looking youths. The general impression which they produced was that of sleek prosperity and success in life. They were all fat, some more so, some less; the young ladies were plump, the elder ones portly. The fresh red faces and sparse grey hairs of the men, their shining bald heads and well-filled cheeks, were the very emblems of prosperous respectability and good-natured self-complacency. They were, moreover, all rich. They had ostrich-feathers, flowers, and fruits in their bonnets, velvet jackets and silk skirts, great gold watch-chains, glossy hats and good broadcloth frock-coats, well starched linen, and a profusion of rings, chains, brooches, and jewels.

For a moment the vision of an Eastern plain, of a swarthy and ragged crowd, with eager, unhappy faces, surrounding a white-robed teacher, floated before my eyes, but passed away like a dream; and in the grey, cold, rainy city where I actually stood, the reality of the white edifice, warmed by its comfortable but unsightly stove-pipes, returned to my outer senses.

At the back of the building was an ordinary table, with a spotless cloth, and on it a cup hidden by a snowy napkin. This appeared to be part of the ritual furniture of the building, but its meaning was not clearly discoverable.

In the oak tulip the comfortable-looking preacher stood, in a black gown with swelling sleeves, reading soberly from a written address, which appeared to be of considerable length.

I listened with attention to his teaching. He explained that in consequence of the sin of the original man the whole human race had become depraved, and that men were born with a curse upon them which condemned them to eternal torment. Not through their own sin, not through any crime individually committed, but merely through the fact that they were born into the world, and that their ancestor sixty centuries ago had sinned in the far-off East. There was no hope, no help for them, however virtuous their lives might be; for, like the Goim of the Jewish creed, Gehenna was their fate.

He told, moreover, of a youthful God sacrificed by the wrath of an Elder Divinity, and afterwards brought back to life and immortality. A deity beneficent to and loving mankind, and one through whose favour—not by any deed of their own, except that of worshipping himself exclusively—men might escape their doom, and be received into an ethereal paradise of clouds and angels. The preacher concluded by recommending the ritual of his creed to the congregation, and by collecting money for the conversion of the Madagascans to this gloomy and paradoxical dogma.

There was evidently no trace of the influence of Rabbi Jeshua in such teaching. The old myth of the death of Tammuz might perhaps be recognised, and the ancient Accadian legends were preserved; but where, in that well-filled building, were the poor and ignorant? The tremendous dogmas were placidly received by the respectable audience, and many of the elder members slumbered comfortably while their pastor fulminated or exhorted above their heads. Could it be that either he who taught, or those who heard, actually believed the strange doctrines which custom had rendered so familiar to them. The sense of unreality pervaded the whole ceremony; and the scene resembled rather the unmeaning repetition of some ancient rite, the true intention of which had long been forgotten, than the living worship of an earnest creed.

But not far away from this edifice was a beautiful Gothic building of elaborate style. Within its shady cloisters, where the ribbed groins of the vaulted roof sprang from the lofty clusters of well-carved pillar shafts, where beams of "dim religious light" were cast across the cool grey stones from quaintly figured windows of stained glass, a service of song was being celebrated, and a thick throng of worshippers was gathered. On the east a gorgeous altar flanked by tapers, surmounted with a painted screen, glittering with gold, with missals, with sacred chalice and plate, was the central object of attraction before which long lines of white-robed choristers stood in order in carved oak stalls.

I looked at the worshippers, and perceived a yet more scanty sprinkling of the male sex. There were graceful and well-dressed women, pale devotees in sombre garb, here and there a sister of charity, or a thin austere ascetic, absorbed in mystic devotion. But where were the poor and the ignorant? The brass plates went round, and I perceived that whereas the previous congregation had restricted its respectable donations to a silver threepence or fourpence, these worshippers placed all manner of contributions in the common offertory. There were pence and halfpence, sovereigns and notes, rings and chains in the plates, and I listened eagerly to hear the good object which had so opened their generous hearts.

An elegant young priest advanced to the choir steps, and announced,

"To-morrow being the festival of St. Architriclinius, the martyr is appointed to be observed. The offertory is for the church flower decorations, and for the fund in aid of providing cotta-surplices for the choir."

Thus I was left to balance the claims of the Madagascan natives against the cottas of the hired choir-boys.

There was, however, still a chance that the doctrine of the æsthetic sect might contain some echo of the ideas of Rabbi Jeshua; and the discourse, which was delivered extempore by the youthful preacher, might contain some indications of the connection.

He commenced with an exposition of the infinite light which shone in the darkness of the universe. He explained the incarnation of the Logos, and expounded the mystic triad of which that Logos formed the active principle. He went on to exhort his hearers to return to the original orthodoxy of the sect as it existed in the fifth century, and extolled the learning and piety of the Byzantine fathers of Egypt, Syria, and Italy.

Now, such dogma was not unfamiliar to me. In the writings of Philo, in the Cabbalistic "Book of

Splendour," I had read the same mystic philosophy as elaborated among Alexandrine Jews; but the new and surprising feature was the importance which the preacher attached to the opinions held by monks and hermits (in one of the darkest ages of human ignorance, human wickedness, and human stupidity), concerning events which had occurred, and doctrines originally developed, more than four hundred years earlier. It was as though we should be directed to search the early Saxon chronicles, as the best and most authentic sources whence to gather a true idea of the history, the religion, and the manners of Rome in her Augustan age.

Evidently, in a creed which thus directed the thoughts and intellects of the faithful to an age of inferior civilisation and less advanced power of thought, there must be some deep-lying fallacy of doctrine which would unfit the beliefs inculcated for becoming a living and growing faith fitted for the wants and the aspirations of an eager and capricious society, in an age of constant change—however suited to the tastes of the time the æsthetic aspect of the ritual might appear.

But there were other gatherings in the great city much frequented, and also claiming exclusive authority in the exposition of things spiritual. In a lecture-room, filled by crowds of intelligent-looking and thoughtful men, I found an eloquent and powerful teacher expounding the great secrets of nature. He explained how, from the infinite mass of formless jelly which floated in the darkness of the ocean, little fragments had become detached; how they formed new desires of their own, and proceeded slowly but surely to adapt their bodies to their fancies, and to follow the dictates of a gelatinous imagination. He taught how the flowers, which desired to attract the attention of certain species of insects, dressed themselves in gay colours for that purpose, choosing the hues most attractive to the particular species they preferred. He stated how he had hunted through the whole body for the presence of any non-material element of life, and not having found any, had been enabled to draw the safe conclusion that none such existed. That life was a function of certain organisms, and that by the exertion of will-force from an almost infinite period downwards, the thinking and moral qualities of mankind had been evolved from the blind desires of the primæval jelly, and his complex organism with its bones, nerves, arteries, and heart, from the simple protoplasm of the bathybius.

A backward disciple here ventured to inquire of

the professor what he considered to be the cause of the very evident difference between a living being and a dead body. The lecturer answered with good-natured contempt that it was clear that the conversion of the vital force, which was the function, as he had already explained, of active existence, into some other mode of motion, would result in the disintegration of the material of the organism into the original protoplasm, or into some newly combined products of inorganic existence.

This answer was so remarkably convincing that no more questions were asked; but the doubt yet remained unsolved in my mind whether it would have been possible for the canvases on which the great Italian masters limned their immortal creations, to have evolved, by any amount of will-force, after any lapse of time, pictures as full of passion, of poetry, of genius, as those which we have received from the hands of the great creators of the art of painting. In like manner, I could not but doubt whether the dogmatic professor could have ever appreciated the infinite beauty, pathos, and dilettantism, if one may be allowed the expression, which is manifested in the works of nature. Nay, even the humour which seems to rejoice in the production of quaint forms, the irony which has caricatured mankind in the monkey, the enjoyment of power and playful fancy which we observe in some of those strange beings which the old pagans rightly named the "freaks of nature."

Is it by the survival of the fittest, or by sexual selection, that these recreations of the creative power were formed? Surely to the artist, or the poet at least, if not to the man of science, it will seem ever less difficult to believe in a Creator who "rejoices in his works," than in this gloomy dogma of automatic organisms.

Suppose for a moment that our professor had been engaged in anatomising a steam-engine. He finds a mechanism of iron wheels, pistons, and cranks, lubricated with oil, and appropriately designed for harmonious action. He decides that by a constant inclination to move along steel rails the primæval lump of iron evolved its wheels, its cranks, its valves; but by his anatomical dissection he has rendered it impossible that the steam-pulse should ever again throb in the great arteries; and he has never seen—or seeing, never understood—the source of life which the Chief Engineer has created in building up the coal in the furnace, and in fanning the living spark of flame, without which the great frame of iron and steel must remain incapable of self-animation—a body with a soul.

Among this hard-headed and narrow-hearted gathering there was no hope then of finding any trace of the doctrines of Rabbi Jeshua. I could only marvel that in an age of free thought and of progress the biologist or the chemist should be allowed to dogmatise not less than the priest or the mystic; and that the illogical argument that because the immaterial was not material, therefore it existed not, should lead captive so many clever thinkers of our day. That flying from the traditional teaching of their forefathers they should fall a prey to the fancies of a naturalist who evolved from the chance production by sea-water and alcohol of a gelatinous precipitate (which he mistook for an organism) the tremendous theory of an enormous jelly floating at an unknown depth in the sunless ocean.

Once more I entered a building where crowds were gathered, and this time it was a picture-gallery. Here, perhaps, among those of gentler and more generous natures I might hope to find disciples of the great poet of the East. But, alas! I was again disappointed. Ghastly enthusiasts with tangled locks and gaunt features, pale damsels with projecting chins limply bending under the burden of poetic melancholy, abounded everywhere. Clinging drapery, quaint headdresses, sickly colouring and ungainly gestures characterised the assembly. They languished before pale, meagre pictures, not less morbid in fancy or less unattractive in design than the admirers themselves might be considered. They fainted at the sight of bright colouring, and shrank before the rude strength of healthful life. Their minds were tuned to a minor key, and they appeared to combine the enjoyment of actual ease and comfort with a delicious despondency concerning imaginary sorrows.

And this is what our fellow-countrymen have become in their attempt to cultivate their æsthetic faculties! The fresh glories of the open field, the sunlight, the storm, the ruddy hues of autumn, the splendour of the sunset, have become too rude and vulgar for the refined taste which can find pleasure only in the decay of the graveyard, and poetry only in the sorrows of sin.

I had, moreover, this difficulty to solve. What became of these sensitive beings if they chanced to suffer from indigestion? or if their boys fought and damaged themselves? Would the contemplation of a gruesome picture console them when a wife or child was laid low with fever? or would an æsthetic wall-paper atone for the loss of a friend?

Therefore, while the languid contempt of these eclectic self-admirers was scarcely concealed as I walked past in the rough dress of an ordinary mortal, I wondered how they could suppose their philosophy of sensuous enjoyment to be in truth a gospel fitted for the needs of the poor, the struggling, and the stricken.

Why! all these creeds, whether it be the respectable religion of the prosperous, the æsthetic devotion of the pious, the narrow materialism of the intellectual, or the selfish dilettantism of the epicurean, are but the religions of the rich and idle, of the men with good coats on their backs, good food to eat, and a balance at their bankers'. These are but new forms of the old selfish doctrines of the rich men of Rabbi Jeshua's age. The comfortable Sadducees, rolling in their carriages, still bless themselves for the rewards of righteousness which they enjoy. The Pharisee still thanks God that he is not as other men, and still points to the tradition of former ages as preserving the epitome of truth. The Philosopher intent on the elucidation of the unknowable, the Epicurean absorbed in his own enjoyment, are not new types of mankind peculiar to our own age.

What comfort to the poor and unhappy is to be found in the dogma of eternal punishment or in the mystery of the incarnate Logos? What consolation to the friendless to know that he is descended from an ape, or developed from a jelly? What satisfaction to the hungry and thirsty to contemplate delicate hues, or listen to the mournful ditties of a world-weary bard? Where, among all these fancies and theories may we find the *religio*, the "binding together" of man to his brother man, the comfort for the miserable, the help for the weak, the hope for the erring, the love for the lonely, which shall form the faith of the people and the consolation of the poor?

Then I became aware that there existed in the great city a division between the rich and poor as deeply marked and as broad as that of the times of Rabbi Jeshua himself. I found that they dwelt in a quarter of their own, a dingy metropolis of labour and want, far east of the broad roads and lofty mansions among which I had wandered. That here, closely crowded in squalid lanes and fever-stricken dens, they lived apart, unknown to and uncared for by the rich multitude of the sectarians; that they knew little or nothing of the manners, thoughts, or deeds of their more fortunate brethren; that they were left an easy prey to the ignorant demagogue or the self-seeking agitator; that their ignorance was abused by men of a better education for selfish purposes, and that the religion of the mass was a creed of hatred and despair.

Here and there a good man wrought and struggled among them by himself, winning their love and confidence, striving to aid their poverty and school their ignorance. Round such men they gathered, as the peasants of Galilee round Rabbi Jeshua of old; yet was it rather in despite of the dogmas which he inculcated than because of the truths which he taught that each solitary apostle of the poor won gratitude and obedience from his flock.

Have we then indeed as a people advanced very far in such matters beyond the races of the ancient world? True, we no longer burn witches at the stake, no longer believe in goblins, fairies, or ghosts, nay even begin to doubt the utility of truth, honour, and virtue, and deny the existence of God Himself. Science has grown up amongst us teaching glorious truths of the methods and economy of nature; but in studying the material we have lost sight of the existence of that by which it is animated, and in cultivating the intellect we have starved the heart.

It was for this reason therefore that the churches were full of women and children, and that the flower of the race was found sitting at the feet of the scientific dogmatist. Religion is a passion, not a proposition of the logician—a need of the heart, not a creation of the brain. Surely those who anticipate a future when art and poetry, imagination and faith, shall be buried in a common sepulchre, and when pure intellect shall reign supreme, have forgotten the healthful and merciful facts that men are born as little children, and are nursed by loving mothers.

It was a little child whom Rabbi Jeshua would have made the religious teacher of his followers; and so long as man is so born, so nursed, the need for a common religion must exist among men. But it is in the wants of the poor, in the yearnings of the unhappy, that the faith of a nation must be found, not in the philosophic dreams of the rich or in the luxurious fancies of the idle.

Thus, as I went on my way disappointed and unsuccessful, I found in the streets a crowd surrounding a child that had lost its father. The black-coated divine from the oaken pulpit passed by and gave a word of advice. "This all comes," he said, "of your sinfulness and perverseness, your disobedience and ungratefulness. You cannot now find your home, and the beadle must take you to the poorhouse."

The priest came by and offered his help, "Flee,"

he said, "to the arms of the Church, repent with fasting and tears, submit yourself to the direction of a ghostly father, and turn from the vanities of the world, and you will be far happier than if you found your parents."

The professor came up, and spoke in a harsh contemptuous voice, "Your father," he said, "was in all probability an ape. His vital force has been translated into another mode of motion, and you will never see him again. You are probably now suffering from the laws which regulate the activity of your organism and impel it to seek the renovation of fuel supplied by food. I judge by the electric discharge from your eyes that some such internal commotion is developing, and I advise you to go and purchase provisions for the regulation of your internal mechanism."

"How sweet and significant is your desolation," said the æsthetic; "how supremely delicious is the agony of such a loneliness. But yet withal how weary must he ever be who is compelled to listen to the griefs of others deafening the music of his own intense content. For this, sweet child, I leave thee to the luxury of woe, lest through too much sympathy I lose mine own delight."

By which of these addresses think you the child was best consoled and encouraged? Where was

Rabbi Jeshua now who had declared once that of such is the Kingdom of Heaven?

Thus to a woman at length among all the philosophers it was left to offer the true comfort, which lay in the simple suggestion to seek and ask for the father who was lost, and to take back the wanderer to his arms.

THE END.

PRINTED BY WILLIAM CLOWES AND SONS, LIMITED. LONDON AND BECCLES.